WORTH IT... $ NOT WORTH IT?

SIMPLE & PROFITABLE ANSWERS TO LIFE'S TOUGH FINANCIAL QUESTIONS

JACK OTTER

BUSINESS PLUS

NEW YORK BOSTON

Copyright © 2012 by Jack Otter

Business Plus
Hachette Book Group
237 Park Avenue
New York, NY 10017

www.HachetteBookGroup.com

Printed in the United States of America

Q-MA

First Edition: May 2012

Business Plus is an imprint of Grand Central Publishing.
The Business Plus name and logo are trademarks of Hachette Book Group, Inc.

The Hachette Speakers Bureau provides a wide range of authors for speaking events. To find out more, go to www.hachettespeakersbureau.com or call (866) 376-6591.

The publisher is not responsible for websites (or their content) that are not owned by the publisher.

10 9 8 7 6 5 4 3 2 1

Library of Congress Cataloging-in-Publication Data

Otter, Jack.
    Worth it ... not worth it? : simple and profitable answers to life's tough financial questions / by Jack Otter. — 1st ed.
        p. cm.
    Includes index.
    ISBN 978-1-4555-0844-0
    1. Finance, Personal. 2. Investments. 3. Pension trusts—Investments. I. Title.
HG179.O838 2012
332.024—dc23
                                                                    2011045289

For Diane

CONTENTS

Every day you try to make smart financial decisions. And every day two powerful, invisible enemies undermine your efforts. The first enemy, I'm sorry to break the news, is you. Specifically, your emotions. The second is the financial industry. But don't worry, together we're gonna lick 'em both.

It took me more than a decade of financial reporting to uncover a surprising fact: The vast majority of financial decisions you face in life are very simple.

Now that statement might sound a little nuts, given the economic picture out there. The stock and housing markets have suffered massive meltdowns, unemployment is rampant, and wages have been stagnant for more than a decade. I'm not suggesting it's easy to get ahead financially. What I am telling you is that there are right and wrong answers to most of the financial decisions life throws at you, and given the necessary information it's fairly simple to figure out which is the right call.

Money is a very emotional subject, and we often get tied up in knots when wrestling with financial questions. Scientists have actually scanned people's brains when they're making decisions about money, and found that the regions that light up are not the ones we use to solve math problems or repair the sink. They

are the ones that light up when people are high on cocaine (tech stocks) or fleeing a **hungry lion** (bear market).

And even when the rational brain does kick in, it often steers us wrong. For instance, we use recent experience to predict the future (houses only go up in value). Unfortunately, recent experience often has no bearing on the future.

So, desperate for help, we turn to the financial industry, which is only too willing to ride to the rescue, charging us for products that are incredibly complex—but that's what we need to deal with our complex problems, right?

Wrong. For the vast majority of your financial needs, the simpler, less confusing, and most important, cheaper answer is the right one.

Most money decisions seem complicated only because someone has a financial interest in confusing you. When you lease a car, for instance, it can be hard to tell how much you're actually paying for the vehicle. That's why the salesman wants you to lease! And car salesmen are nothing compared with Wall Street. There are as many financial products that can part an investor from his nest egg as there are slot machines in Vegas, and there's a broker to sell every one of them. But investors who owned a diversified portfolio of index funds ended the period from 2000 to 2010, the so-called lost decade, with decent gains. Why don't you hear much about this strategy? Because brokers and financial companies can't make much money off it. And besides, when they convince you you're beating the market, it's like doing cocaine!

The pattern repeats itself over and over.

My goal in this book is to help you make the right choice in all these situations. And I've tried to write it to reflect the way we actually face these decisions in life. In reality, we're in the checkout line at Target when we wonder whether to pull out the Visa card and charge it, or use the debit card and pay straight from our bank account.

That's why this book is set up as a series of real-world choices—Is it better to buy a house or rent? Should you give the kids an allowance just for being your kids, or make 'em work for it? Should you hire a real estate agent or sell the house on your own?

Read on for the answers.

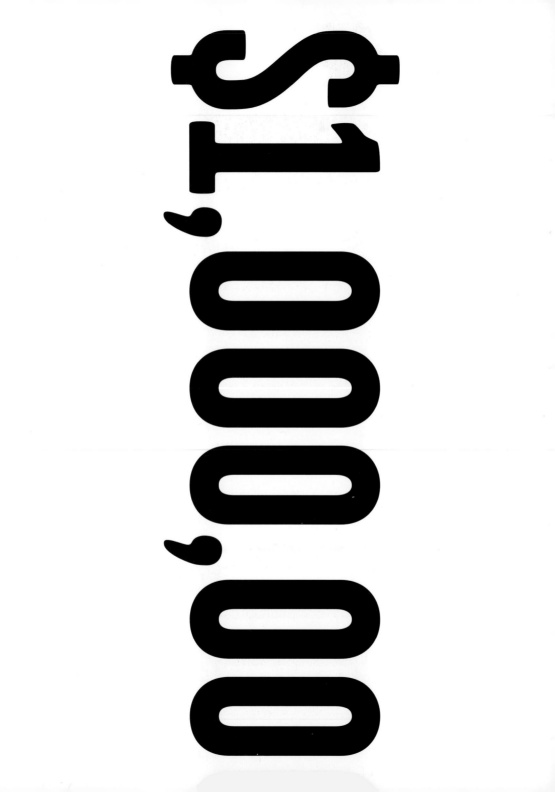

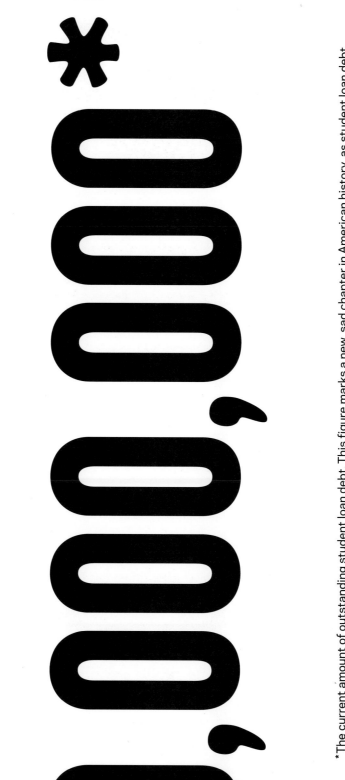

*The current amount of outstanding student loan debt. This figure marks a new, sad chapter in American history, as student loan debt now exceeds credit card debt.

I. GETTING STARTED

MY OWN PERSONAL HOT TUB TIME MACHINE

There are times I wish I could go back and visit myself at 22 or 27 or 33, and take myself out for a coffee (okay, a cold draft beer). Without getting too deep into specifics, my older self would reassure my younger self about the future. My younger self would be slightly disappointed to learn that I am not Paris Bureau Chief, I am not married to a supermodel, and I still fly coach. I like to think that my younger self would be slightly pleased to learn that I have a job that I love, my wife looks like a supermodel to me, I have two great kids, own my own home, take cool vacations, and I drive an old but fast European sports sedan.

My older self would desperately want to pass along some financial lessons, but if I started to talk about topics like "compound interest," my younger self's eyes would glaze over. So this chapter is my attempt to get someone just starting out painlessly pointed in the right financial direction.

People make finance overly complicated, but it shouldn't be. You don't need to run a marathon every morning to get in shape, and you don't need to understand collateralized debt obligations to build a smart investment portfolio. Sure,

there are times that call for professional help. I wouldn't recommend preparing a will on your own, and if you're going to trade stocks—which I don't recommend—you're gonna need a bigger book. But most of the more important cross-roads we all face really can be boiled down to simple one-page, *do-this, not that* solutions.

Unfortunately, The Time Traveler's Ethical Code precludes me from advising my younger self to load up on tech stocks in the 90s and then sell on March 15, 2000, and buy a condo in Miami and sell that in 2006. But to avoid messing with the space-time continuum, I'd just give him advice that's even better—advice that doesn't require a crystal ball. I would tell him to spend less money on stuff, but splurge when it comes to sharing experiences with friends and family. And I would tell him to save as much as he can, and plow that money into a broad portfolio of low-cost stock and bond mutual funds, and hold on no matter what happens in the markets. If my younger self had done that then I still might not be Paris Bureau Chief, but I could take the family—*hmmm*, or possibly just the wife—to Paris whenever I wanted. And maybe we'd even fly business class.

CREDIT vs DEBIT

When the gas station attendant asks "Debit or credit?" use the credit card.

Here's why: Pay with a credit card and the exact amount you charge will get posted to your account. A few weeks later, you'll get the bill. But if you swipe the debit, some gas stations will put a "hold" on as much as $75 in your checking account, and leave it there for a couple of days, until the gas station reconciles its accounts and transmits your actual purchase to the bank. That money isn't available for you to use, meaning you can get hit with overdraft charges for subsequent purchases — even if you have enough money in your account.

CREDIT

And gas station charges are peanuts compared with what a hotel can charge. In addition to the actual costs you will incur—such as the nightly room charge—the hotel will sometimes estimate incidentals (room service, minibar) and put a hold, or "block," on enough cash to cover those expenses. The worst move is to check in to an expensive hotel with a debit card, and then pay the bill at the end of your stay with your Visa. The card-issuing company might hold the block for as long as 15 days, unaware that you paid with a different card. Spend five nights in a $200 hotel room, and, when the phantom incidentals are added in, you could lose access to $1,200 of your own money for half the month.

TAKE OUT A STUDENT LOAN vs SKIP COLLEGE

TAKE THE LOAN

Even while the Great Recession seems to have prodded Americans to increase savings and reduce borrowing in other areas, they are racking up crippling levels of debt to pay for college. Worse, others are performing a quick cost-benefit analysis and deciding it is not worth it.

But as financially painful as college can be, *not* going to college is even worse. At the time of this writing, unemployment was just over 9 percent. But that number masks the education divide: For workers over 25 years old with a bachelor's degree or higher, the unemployment rate was only 4.3 percent.

So really, the only question is: How much college can you afford?

It's far from an exact science, but a good place to start is to consider the earning potential in the student's chosen field. Ray Martin, a New York–based financial planner, ran some numbers: On a $24,000 loan (the national average) with a typical 10-year repayment plan, the monthly payment would be $276 per month for 120 months. By the end of repayment, you would have paid back the $24,000 principal plus $9,143 in interest, for a total of $33,143.

If you're an economics major with a bright future in finance, that repayment schedule is cake. If you're studying to be an elementary school teacher and the district isn't hiring until next year, it could be a stretch. Take cost into account when choosing a school, and focus on the quality of the education, not the prestige of the diploma. **Remember, you can't escape student loans, not even in bankruptcy. But you might be eligible to have a portion of your loan forgiven if you take a public service job.**

So once you accept that student loans are necessary evils, focus on borrowing as little as possible and keeping interest rates at rock bottom. You'll want to stick to subsidized loans. These loans are awarded based on financial need and you won't be charged any interest until you begin paying the loan back as they are "subsidized" by the federal government. Students should look into Stafford loans, which have a fixed, low interest rate and generous repayment options. Parents who want to help can take out a federal PLUS loan.

AVOID A DEFAULT

Check graduation rates at the schools you or your kids are considering. The lower the graduation rate, the higher the student loan default rate. Keep in mind that for-profit colleges have lower graduation rates, and students tend to have larger loans and higher default rates.

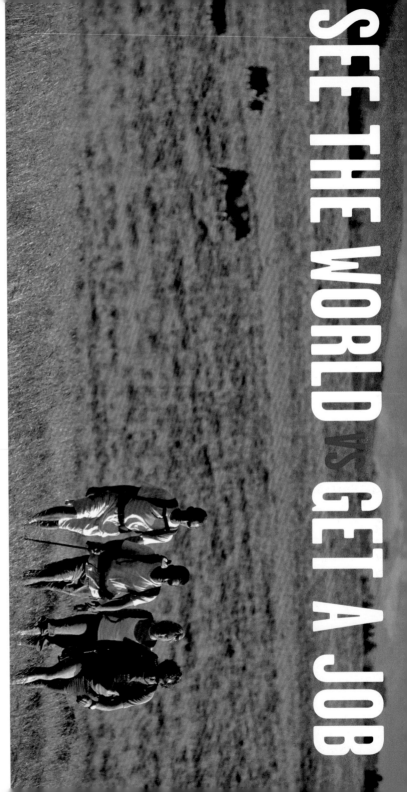

SEE THE WORLD vs GET A JOB

SEE THE WORLD

Much of this book is dedicated to coherent, mathematically sound arguments for getting you to eat your peas. And because much of the rest of your life will be dedicated to eating those metaphorical peas, now is the time for that last fistful of fries. As you reel in the years, the

professional achievements, and the family milestones, you will also accumulate responsibilities. They are all worth it, but they'll tie you down. Even Jimmy Buffett doesn't really live in Margaritaville.

So if you've just graduated from college, you have an opportunity that you will probably never have again. Assuming you can dig up a little cash, you can get on a plane and fly absolutely anywhere in the world you feel like going. Depending on your budget, you can live in hostels or teach English or join the Peace Corps or head to Spain and trek the Camino de Santiago de Compostela.

Sure, there are trade-offs. You'll need to support yourself. You probably won't be starting your retirement savings account this year. Your nose-to-the-grindstone colleagues will have a professional year under their belts by the time you join the firm. And you'll need a good answer for the interviewer who asks what you've been doing for the past eight months.

Why not try telling her the truth: It was, indeed, scary to put your career plans on hold. But, you explain, now that you're back in the U.S., you often think back to that morning, standing at 18,000 feet on the ridge of Kala Patthar at sunrise, when the sherpa's daughter thanked you for building a sewer system for her village. And you realized that before you moved in, the little girl spoke no English, and on that morning she wouldn't stop talking. And you realized it was a once-in-a-lifetime chance not only for you, but for that little girl, too. And you wouldn't trade that moment for anything.

And the interviewer will say: "You're hired."

SPEND IT vs SAVE IT

As a young reporter at a local newspaper, I supplemented my (meager) income by writing freelance stories and shooting photographs for Newsday, which back then was one of the biggest papers in the country. My primary goal was to impress an editor enough to get a full-time job, but in the meantime it was great to get those checks in the mail, for $75, $100, even $150 each. Found money! Which soon became lost money. I must have spent it on something, but I have no idea what.

Whether your long-term goal is a trip to Fiji or an oceanfront condo or a Porsche 911, keep a photo of it in your wallet, in the same slot as your credit card. Every time you think about whipping out the plastic you'll be forced to weigh the purchase against your dream.

BOTH It took me years to learn that I was making a very common financial mistake, which is to increase spending in lockstep with income. In the best-selling book *The Millionaire Next Door*, the authors Thomas J. Stanley and William D. Danko reveal that the key to building wealth is not to earn a lot—many high-earners live paycheck to paycheck—but to spend less than you earn. It's comically simple in theory, incredibly hard in practice, and devastatingly powerful if you can pull it off.

Unfortunately I realized none of this at the time, but late one summer afternoon, after filing a story that I thought was particularly good, it dawned on me that I had absolutely nothing to show for those checks. So from that day on, I saved every freelance dime, and invested the money in a pair of mutual funds. Eventually I got the job at Newsday, and met my future wife there. Those mutual funds were part of our down payment on an apartment.

While it's easy to preach the virtues of saving, it's hard to practice it. One reason is that the pleasure you will get from buying a latte in the morning is so tangible, and yet the benefits of putting the money away are hard to taste. How much will it grow? How will you spend it? Will you even live that long?

So when you get a tax refund, or a birthday check from Grandma, or (if they ever come back) a year-end bonus, try this behavioral finance trick to get yourself to save:

Use a small portion of the money to splurge on something fun. Buy a pair of shoes, or an iPad, or take the love of your life to a fantastic restaurant. **Then put the rest away, in an account you won't touch.**

The splurge is not only fun, it's a way to improve the odds that you'll save in the future. You will focus on the instant gratification of spending that 10 percent, and that will make it easier to save 90 percent the next time a check arrives in the mail.

CREDIT UNION

vs

BANK

Even before the financial crisis, nobody really liked banks. Then they nearly destroyed our economy, got bailed out by hundreds of billions of taxpayer dollars, and thanked us by jacking up fees and refusing to lend money.

So do you really have to do business with them? No! **Credit unions** can do just about everything a bank does, and in almost every instance, they will charge you less and pay you more. On average, credit unions:

- Charge lower fees on ATM withdrawals, loan closing costs, and for overdrafts.
- Pay higher rates on savings accounts, CDs, and money markets.
- Charge lower rates on home equity loans, auto loans, and sometimes mortgages.

The reason credit unions are a better deal is simple—they are nonprofits, owned by their members. They don't pay taxes, and their CEOs tend not to travel in Gulfstream corporate jets. The savings are passed on to you.

While you need to be "eligible" to join a credit union, anyone can become eligible. Sometimes you'll qualify simply by living in the right place, or working for the right company. If not, you can join. **For instance, anyone can open an account with the Pentagon Federal Credit Union, or PenFed, by making a $20 donation to the National Military Family Association, which helps support the families of U.S. servicemen and servicewomen.**

At the time of this writing, PenFed was offering a 1.99 percent rate on used car loans, compared with an average of 5.33 percent for banks. That's a big difference: You'd save more than $1,400 in interest on a four-year, $20,000 loan.

And don't worry, as long as a credit union is backed by the National Credit Union Administration (the credit union equivalent of the FDIC), it's just as safe as a bank. Deposits are insured up to $250,000. In fact, traditional banks took on many more risks than credit unions during the housing bubble, and were five times more likely to fail as a result.

So what are the downsides? Credit unions tend to have few ATMs and even fewer branches, although they may be part of a network that has ATMs in 7-Elevens or drugstores. And their online presence may not be cutting edge; before signing up for a credit union make sure the site is robust enough to meet your online banking needs. I pay most of my bills online; I'm not sure I could go back to the checkbook.

SAVE FOR RETIREMENT

NOW vs LATER

As a 20-something, you have countless advantages over me, a 40-something. Some are fairly obvious, like a full head of hair. Others you won't be aware of until they're gone, such as the ability to go to the movies tonight. (I'll get that back when the kids are grown.)

When it comes to investing, you have an incredibly valuable commodity: time. Time can turn modest savings into a whole ton of money, thanks to the miracle of compounding. The oft-repeated story that Albert Einstein called compound interest "the most powerful force in the universe" probably isn't true, but look at it this way: Physics works against you as you age. Compound interest works for you. The simple magic is this: Over time, your money not only earns interest, it earns interest on the interest. So, like a snowball rolling downhill, the bigger it gets, the more it accumulates.

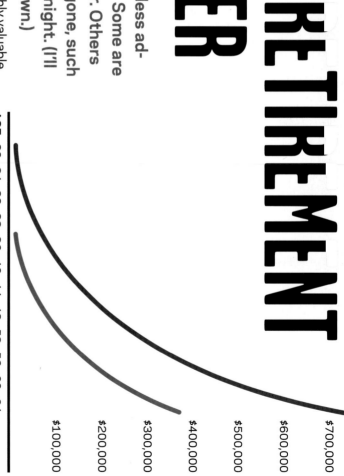

AGE   20   24   28   32   36   40   44   48   52   56   60   64

ANGELINA

SAVES FOR 10 YEARS STARTING AT AGE 20

TOTAL CONTRIBUTIONS: $30,000

AT AGE 65: $749,489.50

BRAD

SAVES FOR 30 YEARS STARTING AT AGE 35

TOTAL CONTRIBUTIONS: $90,000

AT AGE 65: $367,037.60

Let's say you invest $1,000 and earn a neat 10 percent a year. You have $1,000 plus $100, or $1,100. But 10 percent of that is $110, so the next year your savings increase to $1,210. Then to $1,331, and so on. By the time you get to year 40, the annual interest is $4,114, more than four times your entire original investment. (I use the optimistic number of 10 percent to illustrate the math. But it's not as crazy as it sounds: From 1926 to 2001 stocks returned an average of 10.9 percent a year.)

The chart at left shows the power of starting early. Angelina starts saving $3,000 a year at age 20 and then stops saving after 10 years. Brad waits until age 35 to start, and then saves $3,000 until retirement. If their investments grow at 8 percent a year (yes, again I'm being optimistic), Angelina will retire nearly $400,000 richer than Brad, thanks to the extra years of compounding.

I know that in your 20s you feel as if you have no money, but consider this: You have no mortgage, no children, and before you know it, neither of those things will be true. Last year I made 13 times the salary I was paid for my first job. And my disposable income? About the same. Enjoy the hell out of these years. But also put a little cash away. Your 65-year-old self will thank your 25-year-old self.

HOW LONG TO DOUBLE YOUR MONEY

To figure out how fast your money will grow, learn the simple **rule of 72.** Divide 72 by the rate of return—that's how many years it will take to double your money. Expect to earn 6 percent? 72 divided by 6 = 12 years to double your stash. Want to know what annual return you need to double your money in 7 years? 72 divided by 7 = just over 10 percent.

C U
2 NITE?

DATE THE CUTIE IN THE NEXT CUBICLE

VS ABSOLUTELY ANYONE ELSE

There are crimes of passion and crimes of negligence. And then there is falling for a hottie in the office at your first job. That's a crime of opportunity.

It's completely understandable. After four years of college grunge, anyone who cleans up good can be captivating. And once the thrill of setting out on your own wears off, you may be lonely in a new town in a new job. Or maybe you share a passion for, say, long philosophical discussions of why your boss is such an asshole.

I happen to know of a young man who worked at a small newspaper in a resort town. The winters were long. There was a tall, thin woman with long flowing hair. You know the rest. By the time one of you realizes the mistake, the line has been crossed, and the office atmosphere is poisoned. Until someone finds a new job, your workdays will be miserable in a whole new way. **Don't go there.** Remain friends without benefits. If it is meant to be, you will still be friends when one of you leaves for greener professional pastures. Feel free to make sure that her going away party lasts all night.

Now I have a confession to make. I met my wife at the office. I remember little about that job other than the beautiful, brilliant redhead in the orange dress with the daisies. But we were in our 30s, and we'd made enough mistakes to know what we were doing. It was also a big company; had it not worked out, the end of awkwardness was one transfer away.

A relationship built on common professional interests can be a marvelous thing. But when you're just starting out, keep some space between your professional and romantic lives. Both will be healthier for it.

LIVE WITH MUM & DAD
VS GO SOLO IN SQUALOR

DO THE MATH. IF X IS HIGHER THAN ONE, IT'S TIME TO MOVE OUT.

OBJECTIVE FACTORS

Money saved by free rent = 12

Roommates with hot friends = 9

SUBJECTIVE FACTORS

On a scale of 1–10, determine how much pain you would feel in the following situations, and fill in the appropriate numbers in the formula.

LIVING AT HOME

You walk in the door at 8:30 a.m. and have to explain to Mom where you slept.

SHARING TINY APARTMENT

You have to make weekly trips to the Laundromat.

The only home-cooked meals are the ones you prepare.

Each morning you find your toothbrush in a different place in the bathroom.

You have four roommates, but one is an artist, so the utilities are split three ways.

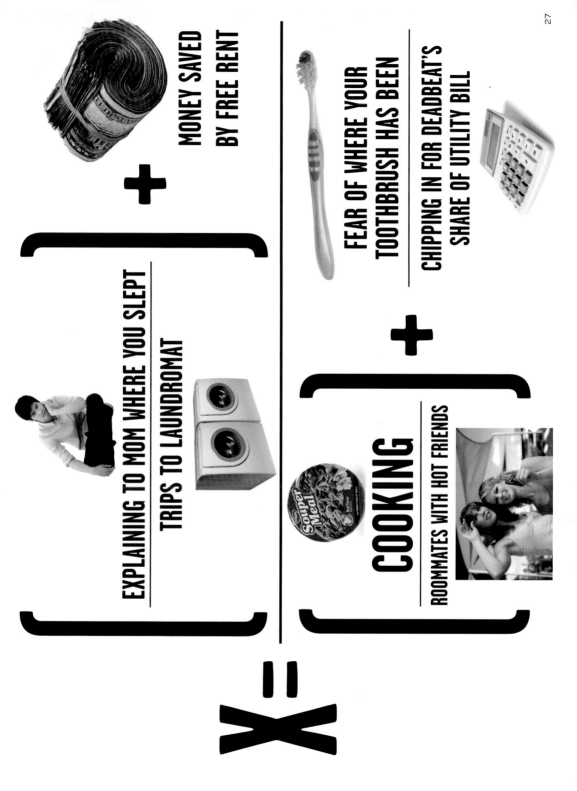

(MONEY SAVED BY FREE RENT + EXPLAINING TO MOM WHERE YOU SLEPT TRIPS TO LAUNDROMAT)

=

(FEAR OF WHERE YOUR TOOTHBRUSH HAS BEEN CHIPPING IN FOR DEADBEAT'S SHARE OF UTILITY BILL + COOKING ROOMMATES WITH HOT FRIENDS)

YMCA VS LUXURIOUS HEALTH CLUB

No doubt you've heard the tired aphorism, "Today is the first day of the rest of your life." Well when it comes to a first job, you really are starting from scratch, and the decisions you make now will determine your financial life. Your basic goal: to live beneath your means. Whatever your after-tax income, you need to spend a little less than that each month. If possible, spend a lot less.

Those first paychecks are incredibly empowering. Someone is handing you all this money, and you get to do whatever you want with it!

STEP ONE

Figure out your financial needs, and add up the monthly cost. Needs include things like rent, groceries, student loan payments, and heat. An iPhone is not a need. Air-conditioning is only a need if you live south of the Mason-Dixon Line. India Pale Ale is not a need, as hard as it is for me to admit that. Retirement savings don't sound like a need, but they are, unless you are sure that by the time you're 65 you'll have learned to photosynthesize. Same with an emergency fund: Unless your dad owns the company you work for, your job is not secure. Oh, and something you need—car, fridge, left leg—will break at some point, and it'll cost you. Now that I've warned you, you can't claim it was a surprise. Set up automatic transfers so you are pumping money into a savings account every month.

STEP TWO

Subtract the cost of those needs from your income. What's left is the amount of money you can devote to that iPhone, a car payment, new shoes, a nicer shower curtain, and, of course, IPA. You'll have to prioritize, and cross off or delay those purchases that you can't pay for with the money that's left over.

INCOME – NEEDS – SAVINGS = MAD MONEY

CONGRATULATIONS

You've just set up a rudimentary budget. That's the quantitative part of the decision-making process, but as with many big-ticket choices you'll be making in the future, there's also the qualitative piece.

Here's a good rule of thumb when evaluating spending options: Open your wallet to pay for experiences, but whenever humanly possible, avoid buying stuff. Ten years from now you won't regret the new couch you didn't buy, but you might have regrets if you stayed home from too many nights on the town with friends.

So, YMCA or luxurious health club? I think now you can figure out the answer.

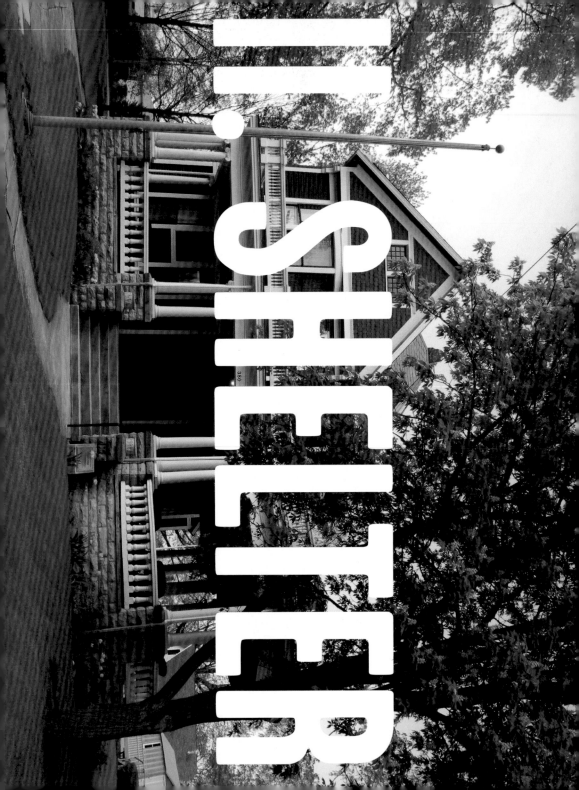

II.
SHELTER

THE BIGGEST INVESTMENT YOU'LL EVER MAKE

There is nothing like the weather immediately after a hurricane. The air smells different. Fresher. The sky is blue. It feels like spring even though it's late August. And then you turn the corner and see that a tree has been ripped out of the ground and crushed a car. The ocean has retreated, but the waves are still huge and dangerous.

This is where the real estate market is today. The disaster has come and gone, and buyers can walk tall. Mortgage rates are so low that people with good credit can practically borrow money for free. Houses are selling for 30 percent off their levels of a few years ago. But the car-crushing maples and angry surf are still there, as foreclosures continue and families struggle with underwater mortgages. (They owe more than the house is worth.)

Where does this leave you? If you are thinking of buying a home, it's a fantastic time. You've got tons of inventory to choose from, sellers will negotiate, and there's no hurry. In a growing number of communities it is cheaper to buy a house than to rent one. Need to renovate the

kitchen after moving in? In a turnabout from the housing boom days, contractors need work now. You set the terms (within reason).

The obvious lesson from the housing bust is What Goes Up Must Come Down. It's a lesson we get taught often, but rarely learn. Still, housing is a very personal decision, and while in the pages ahead I'll tell you what makes the best economic sense, there's a question that only you can answer. It's a question that people should have been asking themselves before the crash, and I hope you'll ask yourself now: Why do I want to buy a house? And do I need one now?

Instead of reflexively buying into the American Dream of home ownership, maybe your personality is a better fit with another American tradition: the frontier spirit. It's a land of opportunity, and you never know where that opportunity might appear. Huck Finn realized he had to "light out for the Territory ahead of the rest." So if you'd rather keep your options open and rent for a while, I bet mortgage rates will still be pretty good when you're ready to buy.

BUY vs RENT

BUY

After an epic bust in the housing market, buying real estate might seem like a moronic financial move. And for some people, it is. But there is one single argument in the buy versus rent debate that trumps all others. As professor Richard Green at USC puts it: You get to live in your piggy bank.

Your parents were at least partially right when they told you that renting was akin to "throwing money out the window." Not because renting is inherently bad—in a perfect world you'd take the money you save every month by renting, invest it in stocks and bonds, and 30 years from now you'd be richer than if you'd bought a house. But it's not a perfect world; we all know you'd spend it on nicer cars and nicer dinners and nicer sneakers and 30 years from now you'd have the same amount of money but no house.

KEEP IT SIMPLE
30-YEAR-FIXED / 20 PERCENT DOWN

When it's time get a mortgage, learn one number and two words: 30-year-fixed. Mortgage rates haven't been this low since GIs were heading home from France. Lock in a low monthly payment and you've just taken a huge step in protecting your family against inflation. Shoot for a 20 percent down payment. Banks will let you get away with less, but we've seen how good banks are at judging risk. With 20 percent down, the chances that you'd ever end up underwater (owing more than the house is worth) are extremely slim, plus, you won't have to pay mortgage insurance.

REASONS TO RENT

SAVE MONEY

Add up the monthly mortgage bill, maintenance, homeowner's insurance, and taxes. Then, even after subtracting the tax deduction, renting is probably cheaper. And that's before you consider the down payment.

FLEXIBILITY

Do you really want to live in one place for the next 10, 20, 30 years? What if you are offered a great job—but it's halfway across the country? Or you get engaged and the love of your life sets one condition—a 500-mile DMZ separating you two from your mother? If you own a home and it has lost value, you face difficult, expensive decisions.

HASSLE

A leaky roof. Ever-increasing property taxes. A backed-up septic system. Are you ready to deal with them? If not, enjoy the carefree life of a renter for a little longer. Houses won't be skyrocketing in cost any time soon.

REASONS TO BUY

FORCED SAVINGS

As we learned recently, a house isn't a foolproof investment. But the requirement to stash that mortgage money away every month for 30 years is a powerful savings tool.

GOOD TIMING

Purchasing a house today means buying a depressed asset with other people's money borrowed at 4 percent—and getting a tax deduction in the process. If inflation picks up, the real cost of that monthly payment will go down while rents climb. Not a bad deal.

PEACE OF MIND

Depending on how quickly you pay off your mortgage, you'll get to live rent-free in 30 years or so. You'll be part of a community. Your kids can use thumbtacks to hang their posters, and you can sit on your porch knowing that the land under your feet and the roof over your head are all yours.

WHERE IT'S CHEAPER TO BUY NOW

Here's how to calculate the rent/buy ratio:

$$\frac{PRICE}{(MONTHLY\ RENT \times 12)} = X$$

If X is less than 15, it's cheaper to buy than rent. The ratios to the right were computed by Trulia.com, a real estate listing and research site.

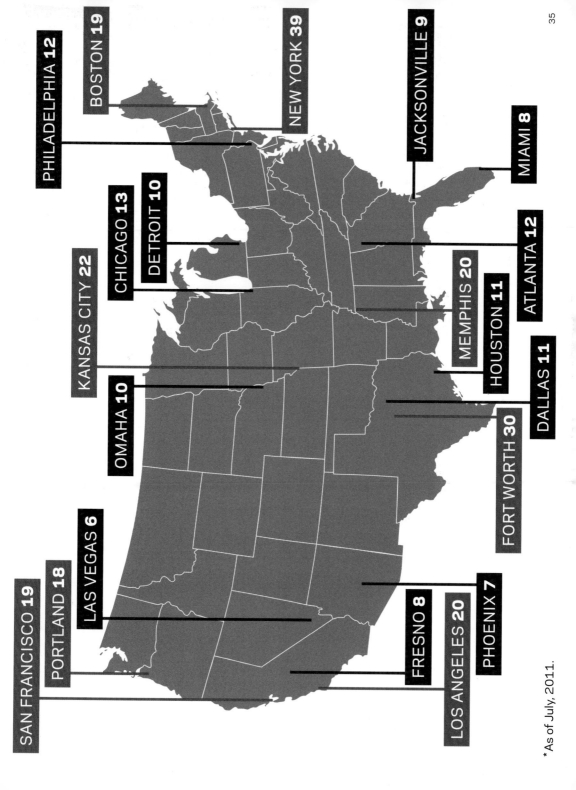

* As of July, 2011.

OLDER HOUSE vs NEW HOUSE

OLDER

Imagine you're debating between two houses—comparable size, comparable location—but one is a charming, old Colonial and the other is just a builder's plan. How can you determine which is the better value? The answer is really a primer in spotting cheapness, and cheapness is easiest to spot relative to other things.

Think back to 1999. Before the tech bubble burst, very few people knew that shares of Cisco and Microsoft and other big tech companies were going to crash and burn, but smart investors noticed that small company stocks (outside of tech) were unusually cheap by comparison. Your crystal ball doesn't have to be crystal clear: Just avoid the expensive and favor the cheap.

As I write this in 2011, there's an anomaly in real estate. After the financial crisis of 2008, builders stopped swinging hammers, and right now new construction is at half precrash levels. Meanwhile, thanks to foreclosures and short sales, there's a huge supply of previously owned homes and a "shadow inventory" of many more expected to hit the market soon.

Thanks to these forces, **new homes are nearly 50 percent more expensive than old ones.** Usually the spread is around 15 percent. Now the forces causing this disparity aren't going away tomorrow, so it doesn't mean previously owned homes are a screaming bargain. But why not go for the cheaper one?

BUT IS NEW FOR YOU?

While you'll pay a steeper premium than usual, you do get some nice conveniences with a new home. Wiring and insulation meet the latest building codes, the layout is modern (closets!), and everything is, well, shiny and new. The appliances are the latest model and might come with a builder's warranty, and if you have a chat with the builder before the house is completed you just might get to upgrade the countertops. But the backyard in a brand-new subdivision might consist of raked dirt, and even if you shell out for landscaping you're not going to get the 100-year-old oak tree that shades the old house on Main Street.

NEW

THUMBS-UP
Insulation, granite countertops, appliances with warranties, closets.

THUMBS-DOWN
Backyard is dirt, trees are three feet tall, and your road has a stupid name.

OLD

THUMBS-UP
Charm, neighborhood, and cheap.

THUMBS-DOWN
Boiler on life support, purple tiles in the bathroom, and when the dishwasher dies, you'll never find a new one to fit in that space.

BEST HOUSE IN THE WORST BLOCK vs WORST HOUSE ON THE BEST BLOCK

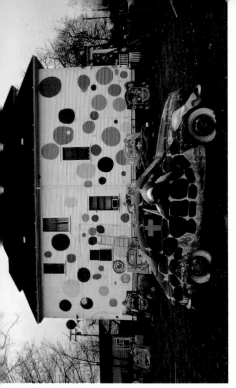

Remember how your mom didn't like you hanging out with certain kids in high school because she was worried they would be a bad influence on you? In hindsight, you know that:

A. She was right.

B. It's the same with real estate.

I don't care how "luxe" the appliances, how "spacious" the master bath, or just how downright "fantastic" the whole package, a bad neighborhood drags down the value of any house in it.

"When you buy the best house on the worst block you're buying what is known as a 'white elephant,'" says real estate expert Ilyce Glink, a syndicated radio host and columnist for CBS MoneyWatch.com. "You set the price for the neighborhood. And no matter what you do to the property, another property will have to rise in value above yours before your property value goes up again."

If, on the other hand, you invest your real estate dollars in the best neighborhood you can afford, even if that means settling for a lesser property, you are setting yourself up for gains in the future. Says Glink: "If you buy the worst house on a great block,

you can improve the house to the neighborhood standard, and the value should rise accordingly".

Appraisers even have a name for it: the "principle of progression." It means that real estate of lower value is enhanced by the proximity of higher-end properties.

To be sure, you may decide that moving to a cheaper neighborhood makes sense for you because that's the only way you can afford the pool or the third bathroom or whatever amenity floats your boat. But from an investment standpoint, the three most important things in real estate haven't changed: location, location, location.

FOR SALE BY OWNER VS REAL ESTATE AGENT

When selling a house, it pays to bring in an expert.

Let's be clear: Purely by the numbers, real estate agents do not justify their cost. Academic studies have shown that hiring an agent will not increase the selling price of your house enough to cover the standard 6 percent commission. Those people who choose the "for sale by owner" route come out ahead.

But in order to sell a house for top dollar, you must be a good negotiator and you'll need patience, organizational and marketing skills, and enough time in your day to take on the real estate agent's duties. Indeed, those academic studies may be influenced by the fact that people who sell their own houses are a self-selecting group of people who have all the free time and skills to nail it.

And today it's a buyer's market, so agents have to work a lot harder than they would have a few years ago to move houses. You're getting more in return for that commission.

Plus, there's an unfortunate, subtle factor you can't control: **Buyers' agents may be less likely to show your house if you are selling it yourself.** Realtors have an obligation to inform their clients of all appropriate listings, but some may harbor a dislike for so-called FSBO properties. In this market, with enormous supply and an overhang of foreclosures, getting more eyeballs on your property deserves a premium.

Here's one situation where it's easy: If you owe more on your mortgage than the house is worth and you have to pursue a short sale, don't think twice about hiring an agent. The bank will end up paying the commission anyway.

FIXED RATE vs ADJUSTABLE MORTGAGE

Why are we even having this conversation? Banks are lending money for 30 years at 4 percent. The last time rates were this low, the cool kids were groovin' to Johnny Mercer and the Pied Pipers singing "Ac-Cent-Tchu-Ate the Positive." These rates are so low that if inflation were to surge, you could actually make money off a mortgage by investing the proceeds at a higher rate. Lock it in, and don't look back.

The trend might continue for a while, but reversion to the mean is one of the few sure things in economics. (A decade later, the NASDAQ is trading at half its all-time high while a barrel of oil has shot up 1,000 percent.)

Adjustable rate mortgages, usually referred to as ARMs, do offer lower rates that you can lock in for certain periods, typically three, five, or seven years, but you take the risk that rates could rise. After the locked-in term expires, the bank can raise the rate as much as two percentage points a year if interest rates have climbed. On a $250,000 mortgage, that's around $3,500 in the first year. Of course you'd refinance before the pain got worse, but you'd have lost the opportunity to borrow at 4 percent.

Sure rates *could* go lower, but here's a good rule of thumb for handling your money: **Any time you see an extreme—in the late 90s stock valuations hit a 70-year high while oil prices hit a 50-year low— don't risk your cash on the bet that the trend will continue.**

WHEN AN ARM MAKES SENSE

Okay, adjustable rate mortgages are absurdly low, too. If you are sure you'll be selling your house in five or six years, a five-year adjustable rate mortgage at 3 percent does make sense. But keep in mind I know a lot of folks whose "starter" home became the "rest of their lives" home. And does flipping a house in 5 years make sense?

RENOVATE THE KITCHEN vs FINISH THE BASEMENT

There are a lot of great reasons to hire a contractor to renovate your house. Just don't pretend it's an "investment." Sure, it's comforting to tell yourself (or your spouse) that your man cave "will pay for itself." But it won't. Remodel because you want a new kitchen, or because sound-proofing the basement will give the kids a place to reenact The Battle of Hogwarts.

Just don't pretend that paying a contractor $30,000 will add $30,000 onto the resale value of your house.

Some projects will come closer to recouping their costs than others. Every year Remodeling magazine surveys 150,000 appraisers and real estate agents to prepare its annual

Cost vs. Value Report. The results are eye-opening. A "minor" kitchen remodeling—defined as about a $20,000 job—returns 73 percent of its cost when you sell the house, edging out the basement-finishing job (70 percent). Aspiring Iron Chefs take note: A "major" kitchen remodeling job ($58,000) is less efficient when it comes to recouping your cost; the magazine estimates you'll get 69 percent back when you sell.

Of course, all these numbers have to be considered in the context of your property. If your kitchen already

puts Martha Stewart to shame, while grown men are scared to enter your basement, the downstairs is obviously a higher priority.

And while it's possible to measure sale prices, you never know what might tip the scales in favor of your house with a particular buyer. Perhaps that come-hither Jacuzzi will strike a subconscious chord, and your bathroom renovation will pay off.

Just remember the bottom line: **Renovate your house for you, not for some future buyer.**

III. AUTOMOTIVE

THE REAL BLIND SPOT

Let's say you are headed to the movies. The ticket price is $10. As you approach the box office, you realize you've lost $10 on the way to the theater. Would you still see the movie? That may sound like a dumb question. Of course you would. Now consider this scenario: You buy a $10 ticket, and then lose it. Would you buy a second ticket?

In an experiment that is famous among people who worry about this sort of stuff, psychologists asked those questions, and 88 percent of the people who were told they'd lost $10 said they'd go ahead and see the film. But only 46 percent of the ticket losers would buy another.

Either way, you're out 10 bucks. Why the different responses? Because participants in the second question feel as if the ticket costs $20, which is more than they'd budgeted for the movies. Behavioral economists call it mental accounting; our tendency to separate our dollars into silos. This is fundamentally irrational—a buck is a buck, whether you put it in the collection plate or blow it on Hummel figurines—but it's how we think about money.

One of the biggest examples of mental accounting may be sitting in your driveway. You may even have a couple of 'em. Most people tend to think of automobiles as a necessity, and they compartmentalize the expense.

They never compare it with other potential uses for the money. *I've got a big family, I need an SUV. Besides, they're safer. If husband and wife both commute, you buy two.*

Here's another way to think about it: A buck is a buck. How many bucks do you have left after you've covered the absolute necessities, such as the mortgage and utilities, groceries, insurance, college savings, basic clothes, and the 401(k)? That number exists somewhere; you need to do the math to determine it. Write it down on a yellow pad.

Now you can decide how to divide up that number. Cable. Dining out. Vacation. Repair the roof. What percentage do you want to use on vehicles? How much money do you want to spend on those SUVs, the extra gas to run them and cost to insure them? As an exercise, imagine the savings if you bought a lightly used, high-mileage sedan for commuting instead. How many family outings is that? Added up over five years, would it be enough to finish the basement? Added up over 30 years, would it mean an annual vacation to Italy in your retirement years?

Maybe you'd rather have the SUV. Just take the money out of the silo and put it on the yellow pad before you spend it.

*The rough amount that customers will fork over to car rental insurance companies for insurance protection next year, according to Neil Abrams, president of Abrams Consulting Group.

NEW vs USED

USED

I've reveled in New Car Smell twice in my life. The first time was the cherry-red Volkswagen Golf in 1991. In 2003, I experienced it again when I inhaled the Scandinavian-by-way-of-Detroit perfume of a newly minted blue Saab 9-3. They ought to be good memories, because those whiffs cost about as much as a Caribbean vacation.

If a house is the biggest expense in most families' budgets, the garage comes next. Spend smart at the car dealership and you'll bank more than you'd ever save by avoiding lattes and clipping coupons. A financial advisor I know compared the cost of a two-car family that buys new luxury SUVs every three years with a household that hangs on to average-priced sedans for 10 years. By investing the difference, the thrifty family could bank $1.9 million for retirement over 30 years.

A car loses a whole lot of value in its first two years of life, and the smart-money move is to let someone else pay that depreciation (preferably a little old lady who keeps it in a garage and doesn't ride the clutch). For example, a BMW 3 Series sedan starts at about $34,000, while a two-year-old model goes for $10,000 less. That's a big discount on a car that is a perennial critics' pick and will still be going strong when Sasha and Malia are in college.

WHEN NEW MAKES SENSE

There are few cases where you will actually pay less for a new car than you'd shell out for a one- or two-year-old one. We saw that in the spring of 2011 as fewer new cars were sold during the Great Recession of 2008, so there was a shortage of cars coming off lease, being traded in, or flipped. Throw in the fact that borrowers often pay lower interest rates when they finance a new car, and you end up with a lower monthly tab for the new one. So run the numbers with an online calculator such as the one at Edmunds.com before you buy. But don't use this aberration as an excuse to spend more!

Buying used you'll also pay less sales tax, a lower ownership or property tax if you live in a state that charges it, and lower insurance rates because the car costs less to replace. If you just love that shiny, spotless new car feeling, shell out $100 or so for a detailing once a year. You'll still end up way ahead.

If you're worried about getting stuck with a lemon, limit your search to certified preowned cars that are still under warranty. It's a pretty sweet deal to let someone else pay the depreciation, but still have the peace of mind that comes with knowing the manufacturer has your back.

LEASE vs BUY

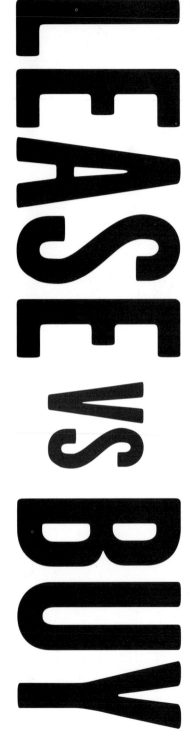

WHY LEASE?

The big exception here is if you can deduct the cost of your vehicle as a business expense, you will be able to deduct substantially more if you lease. Plus, and this is no small thing, leasing is less of a hassle. You're really just renting a car, and since you're getting a new one every two or three years, it won't spend much time in the shop. And yes, less money is coming out of your pocket every month. But that doesn't mean it's cheaper — you're getting less, too.

THE 10,000 MILE RULE

Don't even think about leasing unless you put 10,000 to 15,000 miles on your car every year. However, anything much above that sweet spot and, with most leases, you'll pay a mileage penalty. And if you drive substantially less, you're paying for depreciation you are not causing: You're giving the dealership a gift when you turn that car in with low mileage.

WHEN LEASING BITES BACK

If the car is stolen or you total it, your insurance will only reimburse you for the car's market value, which might not cover what you still owe on your lease. So you have to write a check to the dealer for a car you can't drive. Like most problems, this can be avoided by spending more: You can buy extra "gap coverage" to protect against this.

Buying a car is a better deal than leasing for one primary reason: Once you pay off your auto loan, the car is essentially "free," and the longer you keep it in the garage, the more you save. If, on the other hand, you lease a car your whole life, well, you'll be making car payments your whole life. That great deal the salesman is pitching — Only $199 a month! — sounds like less of a great deal when you multiply it times 40 years.

Leasing a car is like always going to the more expensive restaurant, or making sure you never, ever, pick up an item at the sale price. When you lease, you are essentially paying for the vehicle's loss of value as it ages, what's known as depreciation. And since the biggest depreciation occurs in the first few years, you are in effect always paying top dollar. Plus, your insurance rates will always be at their peak because the car is at its most valuable point in life. If you own a car and hold on to it for 5, 8, even 10 years, it will become less expensive to insure as it ages. Sure the monthly payments are higher when you own, but that's because you're building equity in your ride.

So if buying is a better deal, why are the monthly payments often higher? That's because you're getting more: You're actually buying the whole car, for keeps, not just paying for the depreciation. And of course you can sell it at any time. If you lease, you are locked into a contract, and you're likely to get hit with a big penalty if you have to get out of it.

TAKE THE INSURANCE VS LEAVE INE

One word: **DECLINE.** If you want to be polite, make it "Decline, thank you."

Sure it's a terrifying moment when the Hertz clerk asks whether you want the collision damage waiver and you decline.

The way he'll stare at you, you'd think you just told the pediatrician that your kid prefers Marlboro Reds to those light cigarettes. But do it anyway. Practice it under your breath as you head from the baggage claim to the kiosk.

As long as you have a personal car insurance policy, you should be covered in a rental vehicle. What's more, your credit card probably offers a secondary policy that will pay claims not covered by your insurance.

Just to be sure that you are, in fact, covered, call your insurance agent and your credit card company. The next time you're on the phone with your credit card company and the absurdly polite woman at the call center on another continent asks if there's anything else she can help you with, well, yes there is. She can explain your card's rental car insurance coverage benefits. Ready to take it to the next level? Find out which of your cards has the best coverage, and make sure you use that one for rental cars.

As for your personal car insurance, well, it's probably a good idea to check in with your agent anyway, to review your coverage limits and to ask if you qualify for any discounts you're not getting. Also ask about your coverage when you are driving a rental—and whether the policy covers you when you are on a business trip.

DIESEL vs HYBRID

Deciding whether you're ready to commit Prius-cide or try some of Bavaria's new BlueTec diesels is an easy call with the ALTERNAFUEL-O-MATIC. By breaking down the decision into a few basic criteria (Highway or city? Save money or save the ozone?) you can quickly deduce which car is for you.

WHAT'S MORE IMPORTANT?

PRICE = DIESEL

You'll pay a slight premium for diesel—$1,500 for an Audi A3 is typical—but that's a lot less than the $8,000 difference between a conventional Honda Civic and the hybrid version.

THE ENVIRONMENT = HYBRID

The new clean diesels have come a long way from their smelly forebears, but they can't beat a hybrid, which has zero emissions in electric mode. The Volkswagen Jetta diesel emits 6.8 tons of carbon per year, according to Department of Energy statistics, while a Honda Civic hybrid spits out 4.6 tons.

PERFORMANCE = DIESEL

Would you rather attack the turns on the Pacific Coast Highway at the wheel of an Audi turbo diesel or a Prius? It's not a fair fight.

WHERE DO YOU DRIVE?

MOSTLY HIGHWAY = DIESEL

Cruising at 60 mph, some of the new clean diesel engines will get you mileage well north of 40 miles per gallon. That's not quite as high as a hybrid, but you are unlikely to save enough on gas with the hybrid to make up for the higher sticker price.

MOSTLY CITY = HYBRID

Hybrid engines actually shut down when you're stuck in traffic or waiting at a stoplight. Unlike most traditional cars the Prius is ranked higher in city driving (51 miles per gallon) than highway (48).

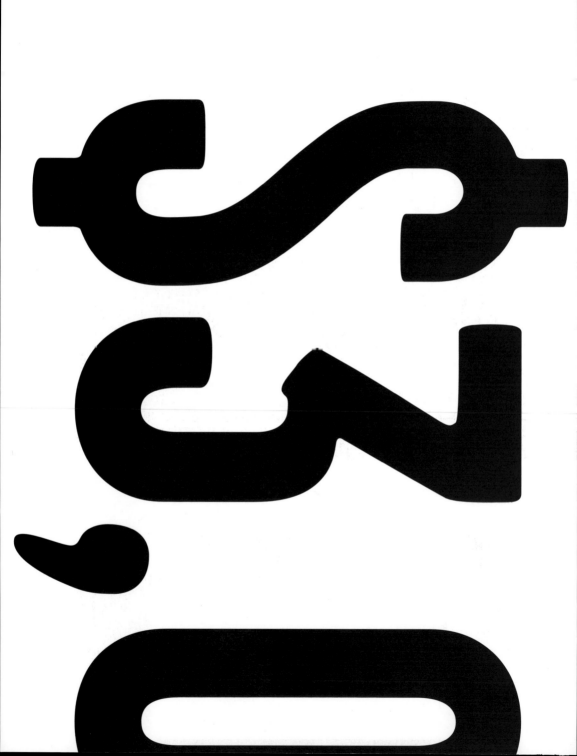

* Roughly the amount a car depreciates every year, before mileage and wear and tear. So when the salesman offers you $2,000 off last year's model, tell him to find another sucker. Start your negotiation at $3,000 off the sticker price.

IV. INVESTING

THREE FLAVORS OF RISK

I've got some bad news that will help you become a better investor: There is no such thing as a "safe" investment.

This certainly contradicts the flyers in your bank advertising certificates of deposit (FDIC insured!), and the guide to your 401(k), which describes the government bond fund as your low-risk option. Here's why:

There are three kinds of investment risk that you must protect your portfolio against: market risk, inflation risk, and emotional risk. And every investment known to man is subject to at least one of them. Market risk is the one that gets all the attention: It slaps you in the face when the market crashes and your stock fund is cut in half. The problem is that if you only protect against that risk, you'll eventually get slammed by one of the others.

Inflation is slower. You'll never see a headline announcing that you lost 4 percent of your money to inflation today. There's no column in your brokerage statement that calculates how much your nest egg is shrinking as your purchasing power declines. But here's an example that might help bring it home: If you are a 30-year-old and you paid the national average for your car, it cost about $26,000. If inflation over the next 40 years mirrors the previous 40, the equivalent ride will set you back $145,000 when you are retired. Invest your retirement savings in "safe" CDs, and you'll be taking the bus.

But the biggest threat to your portfolio is emotional risk. We tend to allow emotions to drive our investment decisions—to sell stocks when they are falling, or buy gold because it is going up. These moves are devastating to returns.

Risk is like the child's game of rock, paper, scissors: You need to mix it up. Bonds are "safer" than stocks when it comes to market risk, but can get clobbered by inflation, while stocks will protect you in the long run.

How do you protect yourself from these risks? Three steps: First, create a truly diversified low-cost portfolio. Second, stick to that mix, no matter what happens in the market. Better yet, set up your account to automatically "rebalance," so that if, say, stocks shoot higher, you pare back your holdings and invest the proceeds in bonds. By going on autopilot, you are automatically buying low and selling high, whereas if you let your emotions drive your decisions, you'll do precisely the opposite.

Third, abandon the idea of beating the market. There are two kinds of mutual funds: active and passive. Invest in passive index funds, which own the entire stock or bond market. Actively managed funds try to pick the best stocks, but over time the vast majority lag the market, partly because they are much more expensive. And by chasing the "best" funds (the ones that have done well in the past), investors end up hurting their returns even more.

THE ULTIMATE NO-BRAINER PORTFOLIO

BILL GROSS

+

JOHN BOGLE

=

Vanguard Total Stock Market Index (VTSMX)
Vanguard Total International Stock Index (VGTSX)
Vanguard Total Bond Market Index (VBMFX)
Harbor Bond Fund (HABDX)

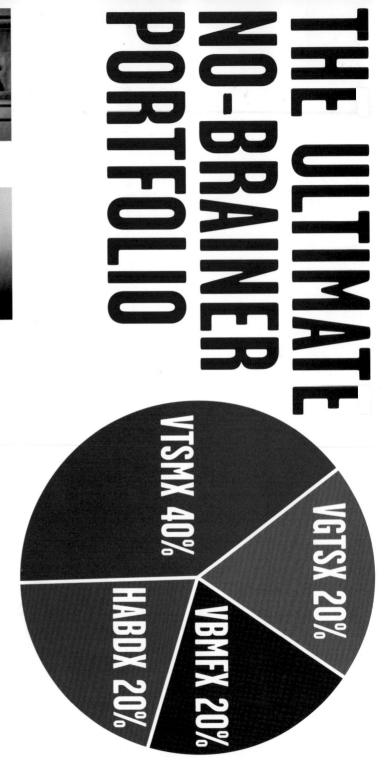

VTSMX 40%

VGTSX 20%

VBMFX 20%

HABDX 20%

This portfolio is extraordinarily simple, and it should outperform the vast majority of investment strategies for two reasons.

One, it gives you exposure to a hugely diverse universe of stocks and bonds, and two, it is incredibly cheap, so you keep your gains, not the fund company. Those gains will compound over the years. It starts with a simple, moderately conservative asset allocation: 60 percent stocks, 40 percent bonds. By investing the stock portion in Vanguard's Total Stock Market Index and Total International Stock Index, you come as close as you're going to get to owning every stock in the world, and you'll pay minuscule expenses. The same logic applies to the Vanguard Total Bond Market Index. If you had owned just those funds from 1999 to late last year in a 60/40 portfolio, you would have reaped a 50 percent return. Yes, a $100,000 portfolio would have grown to $150,000 during the so-called lost decade.

I am departing from my usual indexing orthodoxy, however, to add one more fund to the mix. Instead of apportioning your entire bond allocation to the index fund, I'm recommending you split it between the index and an actively managed fund, Harbor Bond, which is managed by an outstanding bond investor named Bill Gross. You'll pay a higher expense ratio, and Gross will have to beat the index by roughly a third of a percentage point every year to make that up. Recently he's stumbled, and he could do so again. But my logic is this: Bond investors have experienced a 30-year bull market. It's not inconceivable we could have a 30-year bear. Abandoning bonds would be dangerous, but I'd like to diversify my approach by letting a guy like Gross try to find bargains and avoid bonds that look overvalued.

This portfolio is not set in stone. A young investor might choose 70 percent stocks and 30 percent bonds, and as you get closer to retirement you might go 50/50. But if you use 60/40 as your benchmark and only diverge for a good reason, you'll be in great shape.

FINANCIAL ADVISOR vs BROKER

A **broker** is a salesman. Instead of selling cars or suits or pest-control systems, he peddles stocks, bonds, mutual funds, and sometimes insurance products. He is not legally obligated to act in your best interest.

A **financial advisor** is someone who can look at your entire financial situation—from your retirement accounts at work to your credit card balance to your fierce desire to someday own a 1965 Mustang—and help you make it all work. Registered financial advisors are "fiduciaries," which means they are legally obligated to act in your best interest.

ADVISOR

I don't mean to beat up on brokers. Some are really smart, give great advice, and if you're into trading stocks they can be great sounding boards. But the way they are paid means their incentives are simply not aligned with your best interests. Some brokers make more money for selling you certain products rather than others. And usually the cheaper option would be better for you. No doubt some of them will take a financial hit in order to sell you the commission-free mutual fund or the cheaper life insurance policy. But it is absurd to put your financial future in the hands of someone who can only give you the best advice by acting against his own financial interest.

Since you are reading this book, you probably want to make better financial decisions. The best person to help you with that is an advisor with a broad mandate to consider all your financial needs and give unbiased advice. You'll want someone who has the Certified Financial Planner designation (CFP), and a good place to start is the National Association of Professional Financial Advisors (NAPFA). That organization has particularly strict requirements for training, high standards to ensure that the advisor puts you first, and members who work on a fee-only basis. That means they never earn commissions, and therefore have no incentive to sell you one product over another.

HOW TO AVOID THE NEXT BERNIE MADOFF

Whomever you go to for advice, make sure that your account is in the custody of a reputable third party, such as Fidelity or Schwab. Write all your checks to that entity, not the advisor, and insist that statements are sent directly to you. Not only does that drastically reduce the opportunity for fraud, but up to $500,000 in such accounts is guaranteed by SIPC, the government's Securities Investor Protection Corporation. (No, Uncle Sam doesn't rescue you from a bad investment, but he will step in if the brokerage firm goes belly-up or your account is empty and your broker turns up in Cabo.)

BUY & HOLD vs TIMING THE MARKET

BUY & HOLD

In the aftermath of the Great Recession, there has been much chest-beating from professional investors who claim that buy and hold is dead. Here's why the death of buy and hold is greatly exaggerated:

1. Two years after hitting bottom in the worst bear market of our lifetimes, the U.S. stock market had recovered nearly all its losses. Take the hypothetical example of an unlucky, but diversified, investor who put all his money to work on the worst possible day, the market peak on October 9, 2007. If he put 60 percent in stocks and 40 percent in bonds and reinvested his dividends, he would have been up 5.62 percent through November 30, 2011. If it works that well in the worst of times, I'll stick with it in the good times, too.

2. If you don't buy and hold, you have to know both when to buy and when to sell. It doesn't work unless you get 'em both right. And while that's easy in hindsight, it's virtually impossible to do in real time. Even Warren Buffett doesn't try.

There is, however, a way to buy low and sell high. It's called rebalancing, and it's an automatic way to take profits from the assets that are soaring and buy the out-of-favor assets when they are cheap. First you have to set a target asset allocation. If you are in your 20s or 30s, it might be 70 percent stocks and 30 percent bonds. Older investors might go for 60/40 or 50/50.

Over time, as some investments do well and others do poorly, your allocation will change. Once a year you should rebalance your portfolio to get back to your chosen asset allocation. (Some 401(k)s will let you do this automatically.) Let's say you had a 60/40 allocation going into 2006. Since stocks were up more than 10 percent that year, you would have sold some stocks and bought some bonds. At the end of 2008, you would have done the opposite.

So without trying to predict the direction of the market, you would have bought low and sold high. And still, you'd be a buy-and-hold investor.

STOCK vs MUTUAL FUND

It's no contest: mutual fund.

Reasons not to buy individual stocks:

1. The deck is stacked against you. Institutional investors, with their human and computer armies, constitute about 70 percent of volume on the NYSE. That means the guy on the other side of the trade knows more than you do. (And even he usually can't beat the market.)

2. The market is (usually) efficient. In other words, all known information is priced into a given stock. Companies with great prospects are expensive, lousy companies are cheap.

3. Friction: Every time you trade, you pay a commission. Every time you sell for a gain, you pay tax. These costs further reduce the odds that you can beat an index fund.

4. Individual stocks are very risky—so many things can go wrong, even at great companies. Academic studies have shown that you are not compensated for the risk of betting on one firm.

In the most devastating bear market of our lifetime, the market lost 51.93 percent. If you had awful luck and bought a stock index fund at the very peak in 2007, you are more or less back to even now, depending on what the market has done by the time you read this. If you'd bought an iconic American firm such as Lehman Brothers or General Motors at any time, you lost everything.

So does this mean you should never own a stock? No. It just means you should put the vast majority of your stock investments in broadly diversified index mutual funds. Now you can go to bed at night knowing you'll beat 80 percent

of investors. (Less than 20 percent of stock-picking mutual funds beat the market.) Then, if you want to try your hand at trading stocks, create a Gordon Gekko portfolio with a small percentage of your holdings, say 5 or 10 percent.

When the market is crashing or surging, and your instincts are telling you to buy or sell, your gut is probably wrong. But instead of scuttling your nest egg, you can channel those emotions into your Gekko portfolio without doing too much harm. And if you hit it out of the park, great, you've built wealth. At cocktail parties, you can talk about your great trade. Just don't get cocky.

LOAD vs NO LOAD FUNDS

If you buy a mutual fund through a broker, you may have no choice but to pay a sales commission or "load," which can be as high as 5.75 percent. That means that if you invest $10,000, only $9,425 actually goes into the fund. The fund needs a gain of 6.1 percent just to get you back to even. And if it carries the average 1.3 percent expense ratio for actively managed funds, make that a first-year gain of 7.4 percent before you actually earn a penny.

NO LOAD

Given how hard it is to beat the market, starting at such a disadvantage is like tying your shoelaces together before starting the race. Oh, and actively managed funds tend to trade frequently, which can result in a tax hit and drive up hidden costs. To be sure, if you hold the fund for many years, the impact of the load is greatly reduced, and a few portfolio managers beat the index by more than they charge in fees. But the more you know about mutual funds, the better low-cost indexes start to look. Why start with all those disadvantages?

As I suggested earlier in this chapter, I believe the vast majority of investors are better off with a fee-only advisor rather than a broker. The fee-only guy certainly isn't free, but when you put $10,000 in a no-load fund, your full 10 grand will go to work for you.

If, on the other hand, you do find yourself restricted to the load-fund universe, look for fund companies that put shareholders first by charging below-average expense ratios, trading infrequently, and telling you how much of the portfolio managers' wealth is invested in their own funds. Among the organizations with good track records are American Funds and the Davis Funds.

LOAD FUND OPTIONS

If you have to buy a load fund, here are three good ones, recommended by Russ Kinnell, director of fund research at Morningstar:

ANWPX
American Funds New Perspective
Holds foreign stocks; great long-term record

NYVTX
Davis New York Venture
Mostly U.S. stocks; treats shareholders well

TPINX
Templeton Global Bond
Volatile but high returns; good diversifier

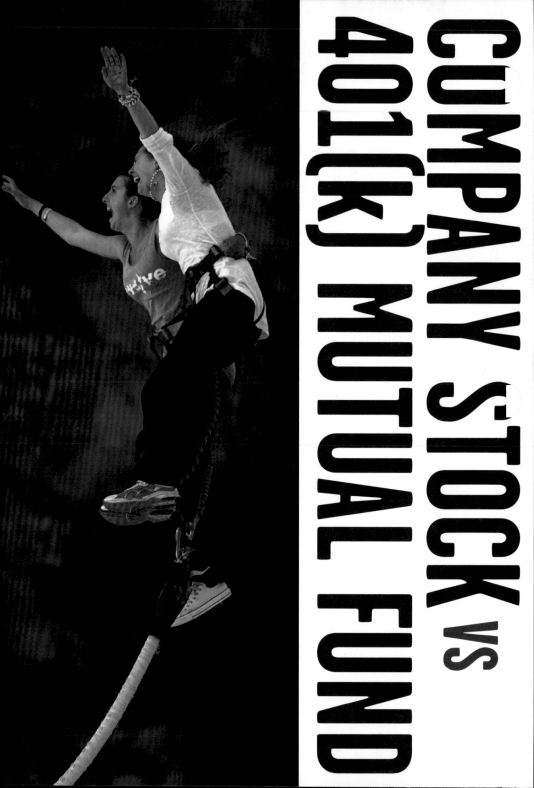

COMPANY STOCK vs 401(K) MUTUAL FUND

MUTUAL FUND

Let's say you have to bungee jump into the Grand Canyon. At night. It's windy. (Bear with me here.) That's the bad news. The good news is that you have a choice of harnesses. The first one consists of a single bungee line. We're going to call it your company. The second includes not only your company's line, but also a bunch of backup lines of varying materials, some of them thicker and stronger than your company, and a harness that attaches to your body in more places . . . .

I don't need to finish the question. Your answer is "Duh." So then why on Earth would you tie your financial security in retirement to the fortunes of a single firm, the very same firm upon which you rely for your income and your health insurance and those annual trips to the sales meeting in Vegas? In the event, as unlikely as it may be, that something awful should happen to your employer, you not only lose your job, your health insurance, and that sweet suite at Caesars Palace, but your entire retirement plummets into the abyss, too. Do you know, beyond all shadow of a doubt, that your CEO is a Boy Scout? Would you trust the CFO to take care of your baby for a week?

Seriously, of all the incredibly simple steps you can take to avoid a worst-case financial scenario, keeping a minimum of your 401(k) in company stock is a real easy call. And yet, according to the most recent numbers from the Employee Benefit Research Institute, 28 percent of employees who had a company stock option in their retirement plan had plowed more than 20 percent of their savings into their firms' shares. I don't care what a great company you work for. Enron and AIG and Lehman Brothers and Arthur Andersen were great firms once, too.

Diversify. Today.

HOT FUND vs CHEAP FUND

Here's a secret that the financial industry really doesn't want you to know: The cheaper the mutual fund, the better it is.

How great is that? With cars, you usually have to pay more to get more. You may think BMWs are overpriced, but you gotta admit that you'd rather drive an X5 than a GMC Acadia. Generic ibuprofen is the same medicine as Advil, but at least you get that nice coating on the name brand.

With mutual funds, it's the opposite. The single best predictor of a mutual fund's future performance is fees. The lower they are, the better your returns. A study by Morningstar found that the cheapest funds outperformed the most expensive funds 100 percent of the time. Great returns last year, meanwhile, don't tell you much about how a fund will perform this year.

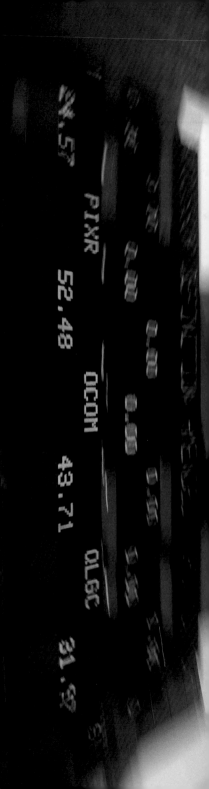

There are lots of reasons that cheap funds do better, including the fact that when fund companies charge less, it means they put investor interests ahead of their own. Fundamentally, the more they take, the less you keep.

Let's do the math: Active investors pay an average of 1.3 percent a year in fees, or $13 for every $1,000 invested, plus hidden costs from trading that can take the total past 2 percent. Meanwhile some index funds charge fees as low as .07 percent, or 70 cents. And they hardly ever trade.

That $13 doesn't sound like much, but the pernicious effect compounds over time so more and more of your return is eaten up with fees. With the difference, you could literally take a vacation to Europe every year in retirement.

WANT AN EXTRA $507,480 IN RETIREMENT SAVINGS?

Consider a 30-year-old couple with a combined $100,000 in their retirement accounts, and assume 8 percent annual returns before expenses and no further deposits. If they pay an expense ratio of 1.3 percent, or $1,300, they will hit age 65 with $935,258. Not bad. But what happens if they invest that money in a low-cost index fund and pay 0.07 percent in fees? They retire with $1,442,738 in the bank. Yes, that $1,300 translates into more than half a million dollars in fees, plus earnings they would have banked if they hadn't paid out those fees. Run your own investments through an online calculator; you'll be shocked at how much you can save by investing in low-cost index funds.

And you'll understand why fund companies don't want you to know this secret. They'd rather keep that half a million bucks for themselves.

OUTSTANDING LOW-COST FUND OPTIONS

Vanguard Total International Stock Index Fund Admiral Shares (VTIAX) expense ratio: 0.20%

Fidelity Spartan Total Market Index Fund (FSTMX) expense ratio: 0.10%

Schwab U.S. Aggregate Bond ETF (SCHZ) expense ratio: 0.10%

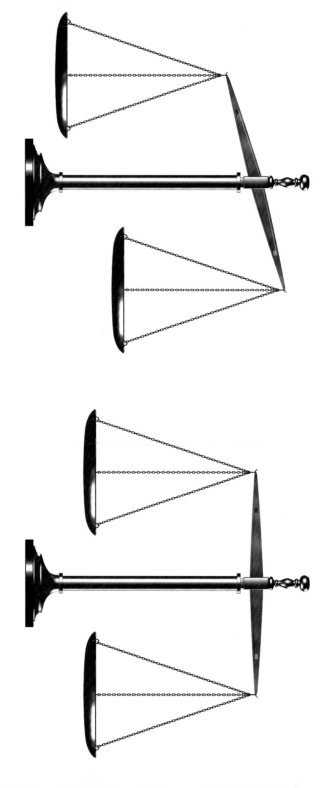

CAP-WEIGHTED INDEXING
vs FUNDAMENTAL INDEXING

This is nerdy but important information if you're investing in index funds. These low-cost investments are tax efficient and give you virtually the entire return generated by the stock market.

But there is a downside. The stocks in an index are weighted by market value, or "capitalization," which means that the more a company's stock market value increases, the bigger the stock's representation in the index. If you own an index fund, chances are its holdings are weighted the same way. So, for example, Exxon constitutes 3.5 percent of the Vanguard S&P 500 fund, while Walmart is 0.84 percent. **When investors get irrational and pour money into a hot stock, the index is forced to go along for the ride.** As Internet stocks soared to outrageous heights during the 1999–2000 bubble, the index was more and more heavily weighted toward WorldCom, Global Crossing, and other companies whose rising share prices were based on hope (and hype) rather than value.

"With cap weighting, you're assuming that a stock's prospects are better after it's soared than before it soared," Robert Arnott told attendees at an investing conference in 2010. Arnott, a former editor of the prestigious *Financial Analysts Journal*, thinks he's found a cure. He is a pioneer of "fundamental indexing," an approach that seeks better ways of ranking companies than their market value.

Arnott's company, Research Affiliates, offers index funds whose components are ranked by measures such as sales and dividends. Competitors, such as Jeremy Siegel's Wisdom Tree, favor earnings over sales, but the common idea is to use a measure that is grounded in fundamentals, rather than the market's mood.

So should you own these funds? They are a fine way to diversify your holdings, but there isn't sufficient evidence that they should replace your core holdings of traditional index funds. Really, they are just a new form of active management. Any time you change the yardstick for measuring the value of a company, you make an investing decision. So if dividends are important, you are choosing Pfizer over Apple. If you consider the number of employees, then GM is favored over eBay. There are periods when the market will reward those choices, and times when it will punish them.

In June 2010, Arnott pointed out that Apple was becoming an ever larger component of the market by stock value, and suggested that its smaller share, in a fundamental index, would give index investors a more rational exposure. A little over a year after he said that, the market was up 20 percent and Apple was up 40 percent. He may yet prove correct, but so far it hasn't panned out that way.

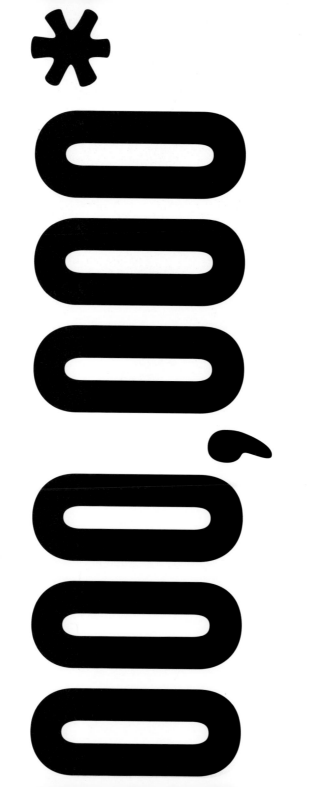

* Estimated fees paid plus earnings sacrificed by investors in actively managed mutual funds that have underperformed the market over the past decade.

INDIVIDUAL BONDS vs BOND FUND

Believe it or not, this is a hot debate among financial advisors. Two colleagues of mine got so worked up over the topic that we had to intervene before they came to blows. (Memo to self: Need to meet some new people.)

BOND FUND

Bottom line first: If you are investing on your own (or found math homework challenging), use mutual funds to get your bond exposure. It's just not cost-effective to try to buy bonds on your own. As always, a low-cost index is a great way to go.

Why is this even a debate? Because bonds are very sensitive to interest rates. When rates rise, existing bonds *fall* in value. Why? Consider this example: If you own a $1,000 Treasury bond that pays 4 percent interest and matures in 10 years, you get $40 a year in interest and you get your $1,000 back in 10 years. If rates rise to 5 percent, however, investors are not going to pay $1,000 for that 4 percent bond. Why would they when they can get 5 percent for the same investment? You'll still get your money back if you wait 10 years, or you can sell the bond for $800, because at that price the $40 payout amounts to the going rate of 5 percent.

Now if you own that $1,000 bond in a mutual fund (and intrest rates rise), it's more complicated. The value of the fund is going to fall to reflect the new, lower value of that 4 percent bond. And since funds are constantly buying and selling bonds, there's no equivalent of holding to maturity. If rates keep rising, you might have to sell your share in the fund at a loss. (While the fund will benefit from the bigger payouts of the new, higher yielding bonds, there's no guarantee those payouts will make up the difference.)

Because of this danger, some advisors would prefer you to buy individual bonds, knowing their clients will get their full principal back. Most individuals will be charged such large markups on bond purchases that it's not cost-effective to buy them, but money managers can buy in large enough blocks that they can negotiate a better price. And bonds can serve useful purposes: Say you plan to retire in five years, and you expect you'll need $20,000 in living expenses above and beyond Social Security. Your advisor can buy a $20,000 bond that will mature in that year, guaranteeing that the cash will be there when you need it, with no risk of selling at a loss.

HOW TO GET YOUR BONDS ON

1. The Vanguard Total Bond Market ETF (BND) charges a mere 0.11 expense ratio and gives you exposure to U.S. Treasuries, corporate bonds, mortgages (safe ones), and even a smattering of foreign bonds.

2. While it's tough to go wrong with an index fund I suggest that you consider diversifying your bond holdings by owning an actively managed fund such as Harbor Bond Fund (HABDX). The investing decisions are made by Bill Gross, who manages the better-known PIMCO Total Return Fund, but the Harbor fund has much lower expenses and no load, or sales charge.

ETFs vs MUTUAL FUNDS

ETFs are a lot like a **single-barrel bourbon:** They should be used in moderation. In fact, if you're asking whether to buy an ETF or a mutual fund, you may be asking the wrong question. Choosing an appropriate asset allocation and minimizing costs are far more important than which type of investing vehicle you use.

First the background: ETFs, or exchange-traded funds, are a fairly new financial invention—they were first introduced less than 20 years ago and only really caught fire over the past decade. Total ETF assets passed the $1 trillion mark in 2011. Like mutual funds, they are a basket of assets such as stocks or bonds. But unlike funds, they trade on an exchange like a stock, and so the price varies throughout the day. Mutual funds, which you buy from the fund company, are priced at the end of the day based on the closing prices of the underlying bonds, shares, or whatever the fund owns.

Generally, ETFs track indexes, though some companies have begun to market actively managed versions.

Here's the most important thing to understand about ETFs: Used properly, they have slight advantages over mutual funds in some instances. But there are also many more opportunities to do mischief.

The Good: The best ETFs have low fees, and they are tax efficient—you don't pay Uncle Sam until you sell them for a gain. But the best index mutual funds have fees that are the same or only marginally higher, and the well-managed ones rarely pass on capital gains.

The Supposedly-Good-But-Not-Really: Fans will tell you that ETFs are great because you can trade them all day. Woo-hoo! Here's what that means in real-world terms: My colleague Nathan Hale at *CBS MoneyWatch* compared the returns of ETFs with equivalent mutual funds over a five-year period and found they were virtually identical. But the actual returns for the ETF investors were four percentage points worse. How could that be? Because they traded in and out so frequently. And trading is a surefire way to lose money.

The Bad: Since ETFs trade like stocks, you pay a commission when you buy or sell them. If you are regularly putting money in an account, aka dollar-cost averaging, those commissions will eat into your returns. Some firms offer commission-free ETFs; just make sure their expense ratios don't outweigh the savings.

The Really Bad: Just as *Jaws 3-D* was an embarrassment to the franchise, some of the newer ETFs amount to an abuse of a good idea. Cheap, tax-efficient exposure to a broad index was a good idea. But then, driven by marketing, financial firms started creating indexes just so they could sell a fund based on them. There are now more than 1,000 ETFs. Should you really bet your nest egg on the palladium market or the Russian ruble? And stay far away from leveraged funds, which may have their place in a professionally managed portfolio, but can wreak havoc faster than you can say "You're gonna need a bigger boat."

LEVERAGED VS UNLEVERAGED ETFS

DON'T TRY THIS AT HOME.

A new breed of exchange-traded funds aims to double or triple the daily return of a benchmark through leverage (borrowing). So, for example, if the fund tracks the S&P 500 and it goes up 2 percent in a day, you get 4 percent. Of course if it goes down 2 percent, you're down 4. But if you've been paying attention while reading this book, it won't surprise you to learn that financial firms have an answer for that problem—the inverse fund! If you expect the market to fall, you can buy a fund that aims to double or triple the *inverse* of its return. The market falls 2 percent? You're up 4 percent!

There are two reasons to treat leveraged funds like the financial equivalent of *Jackass* stunts.

1. You don't know what the market is going to do tomorrow. No one does. This is gambling, not investing. You have a 50/50 chance of guessing correctly, but these funds actually punish you more for getting it wrong than they reward you for getting it right—and that leads to the second problem.

2. The math of these funds is cruel. Say you invest $1,000 in a 2x leveraged ETF. If the market jumps 10 percent tomorrow, your investment is worth $1,200. Then it falls 20 percent the next day, and you're down to $720. The next day the market climbs 15 percent, and your stake rises to $936. Had you invested the $1,000 in an equivalent un-leveraged fund, you'd have $1,012, a $12 gain. But instead of making you $24 richer, the leveraged fund made you $64 poorer.

Obviously those swings are exaggerated, but they illustrate the problem of leverage: Hold the fund for more than a day, and your returns deviate farther and farther from the market.

There may be reasons for a professional trader to use these things, and that's just fine. Professional drivers may take your car deep into the triple digits on the test track. That doesn't mean you should do the same on the highway. Especially not with your family in the backseat.

2-YEAR CD vs 7-YEAR CD

GO LONG

If you might need access to your money in two years, you're probably reluctant to lock it up in a seven-year certificate of deposit. And what happens if interest rates shoot higher? Will you be stuck in that awful low-yielding investment for the rest of the decade?

Surprisingly, the seven-year is far and away the better deal, as long as you get the right CD. Here's why: At the time of this writing, the best seven-year CD is yielding 3.4 percent and has an early withdrawal penalty of 12 months. The highest yielding two-year CD is paying 1.55 percent. So if you hold it to maturity, you'd earn $310 on a $10,000 investment. If, instead, you purchase the seven-year and pull your money out after two years, you'd earn $340 after the penalty.

But even the two-year CD yielding 1.55 percent is a great deal compared with the alternative. For comparison's sake, a two-year Treasury note yields only 0.26 percent. The only reason you can get a CD yielding nearly six times as much as an equivalent bond is that financial institutions can't invest in CDs. CDs are not

available—or insured—in the huge amounts they are putting to work. (If institutions could take hundreds of billions of dollars out of government bonds and pour them into CDs, short-term Treasury prices would rise and CD rates would fall.)

Amateur economists take note: Getting a risk-free return that is six times higher than the government bond alternative is about as close as you are ever going to get to a free lunch.

TIMBER vs GOLD

Gold fever is spreading. The shiny metal is up six-fold over a decade in which stocks did squat, real estate got slammed, and the economy fell off a cliff. The Jeremiahs of financial doom tell us that our paper money (or "fiat money" as they call it) will be worthless and that our salvation lies in the return of the gold standard.

So what has been a better investment over the past 30 years, gold or stocks? It's not even close. My colleague Allan Roth, a Colorado financial advisor, invested $3,320 in gold in 1980, during the last gold fever. His investment is now worth around $7,500. Adjust for inflation and he's actually lost money (but still will owe taxes on his "gain"). Had he put that three grand in the stock market, he'd have more than $100,000 today.

I don't know where gold will go from here; perhaps it will keep on rising. And there's nothing wrong with having a small allocation to gold in your portfolio (2 to 5 percent, maximum), because when investors are scared, and selling everything else, they are often buying gold.

But here's another idea: Instead of buying the asset that's climbed sixfold in the past decade, how about an investment that some say is better protection against inflation over the long term, but hasn't had such a run-up of late? I'm talking about timber.

Unlike gold, trees grow. There are no huge deposits that might be discovered, lowering the price of existing trees. And demand is unlikely to go away. Sure, gold is used in teeth, jewelry, and as paint in a famous James Bond scene, but wood builds houses, perhaps the chair you're sitting in, and, until predictions of a paperless society prove more accurate, endless reams of paper.

In a book preaching the virtues of index investing, warning you away from stock picking, market timing, and fad following, why would I devote space to comparing gold with timber? For starters, something has to go in the gambling portfolio. But even if all I do is make you think twice before following the herd into gold, I've done my job.

HOW TO BUY WOOD

Pension funds and hedge funds discovered the virtues of investing in forestland decades ago, and while buying your own hundred-acre wood might be a little pricey, you can get exposure via real estate investment trusts, such as Plum Creek Timber (PCL). Unlike most REITs (not to mention savings accounts) the interest is taxed as long-term capital gains, not ordinary income, so you get to keep more of Plum Creek's nearly 5 percent payout.

V. FAMILY MATTERS

THIS IS YOUR BRAIN ON CHILDCARE

About 10 years ago I got some great advice from a source that, according to popular culture, is not a place where men usually go for counsel: the mother-in-law. She told me that if you wait until you're "ready" to have children, you'll never have children at all. Her wisdom: You can't actually prepare—parenthood is utterly unpredictable and you simply have to take the leap and then improvise.

Sure enough, when our daughter Lily arrived on the scene, we had the crib, the adorable onesies, *What to Expect When You're Expecting*... and we were gloriously unprepared. Perhaps the biggest change was the non-stop nature of parenting. Even marathons have finish lines, but this little bundle was always demanding attention. On those seemingly rare occasions when she actually slept, my wife figured something must be wrong, and would ask me to sneak into the nursery to "make sure she's not dead." Now Lily is eight, her brother is five, but I still tiptoe into the children's room almost every night before bed to check on them. I am always struck by their angelic sleeping faces, and by the fact that their non-stop minds and bodies (and voices!) are finally still.

It's not only a nice peaceful moment; it's a reminder of the importance of getting off the roller coaster once in a while to check up on things. As parents trying to hold down jobs, run a household, and occasionally clean that mystery substance off the Legos, it's easy to let a few

things slide. The beneficiary designation on your 401(k) is something you're forever meaning to deal with but never get to. This chapter should help you take a few easy steps to improve the family finances. Especially those things that don't seem important—until they are.

In the past few years I have seen two fathers—healthy, athletic guys—die in utterly unpredictable accidents. They each left a wife and two children. Mortality is no fun to think about, but the cost of inaction is simply too high.

Your first job is to make sure you are covered in the case of catastrophe. Hire an attorney to draft a will. And we'll cover disability and life insurance in the pages that follow.

Your second job is to challenge your financial preconceptions. Would a vacation be more valuable than a new car? Do you need organic cookies? Okay, you're probably not stressing over that last one. Rather than accepting your monthly bills as the cost of running a household, why not look at everything with a fresh eye?

Oh, and make sure you check your 401(k) beneficiaries. I've heard too many stories about young men who, for lack of any other candidates, put down their girlfriend's name and never bothered to update it. I'm sure she was a nice girl, but you've got other priorities today. I hope those priorities are sleeping peacefully right now.

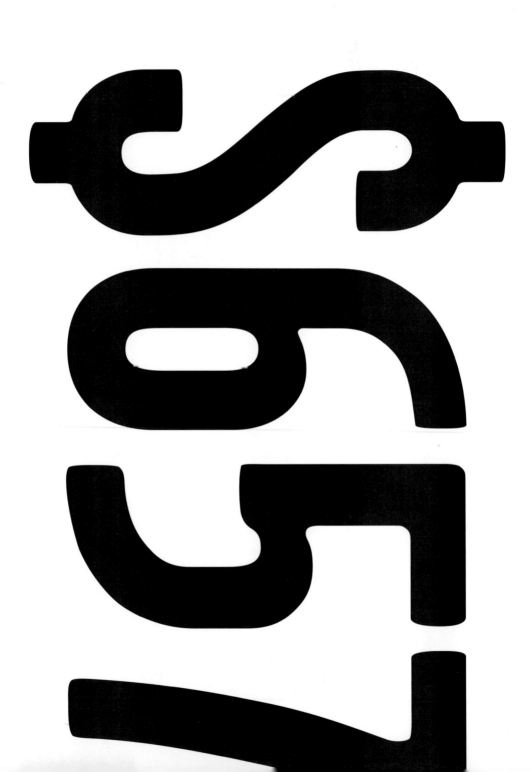

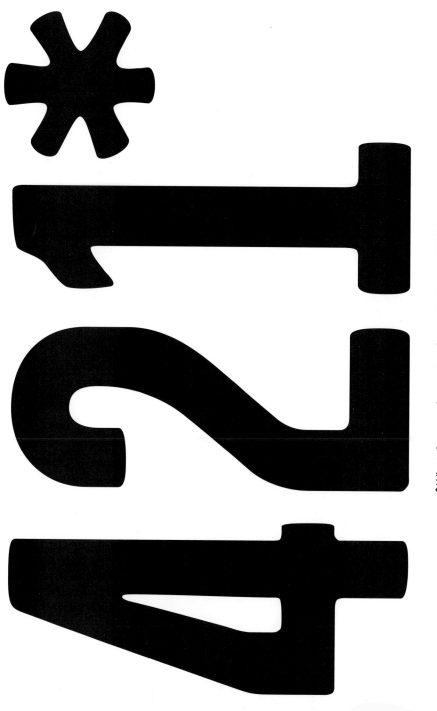

*What the proud parents of a genius born in 2012 can expect to pay for that child's Harvard diploma in 2034.

529 PLANS vs UGMAS

529

It's no secret that the cost of a college education has been rising at an obscene rate, much faster than inflation, for years. But until you do the math, until you see all six digits that you will be responsible for, the awesomely painful reality may not have set in. Eighteen years from now even the average public college will be charging $254,000 when you include tuition, room and board, and incidentals.

Sure, financial aid will help in a lot of cases. Indeed, the *Harvard Crimson* reports that more than 60 percent of students there get some form of aid. But clearly, the average mom and dad are going to have to save until it hurts. Luckily, the best savings vehicle known to man is available for this purpose: the **529 plan.**

A 529 is an educational savings account, run by a school or a state, designed to help parents (of all incomes) to set aside money for college costs. **When you save money in a 529, you pay no state or federal taxes on the gains—ever—as long as you use the money for college.** What's more, some states, including Illinois, New York, and South Carolina, offer a tax deduction for contributions. There are no other savings vehicles that offer tax-free growth on deductible contributions.

Here's the savings vehicle you don't want: An **UGMA,** or uniform gift to minors account. These complicated creatures allow parents to put money in a child's name to save on taxes. But among their many drawbacks, they are counted as the child's asset under financial aid formulas. A 529 is considered the parent's asset.

Here's why that's important: Financial aid formulas assume a certain percentage of your savings are available to pay for college. For students it's a maximum of 20 percent of assets, for parents it's 5.64 percent. Plus, the formula exempts some savings; the number gets larger according to the age of the oldest parent. So, for example, a 55-year-old with $100,000 saved would get an exemption of about $60,000. So student aid would be reduced by just 5.64 percent of the remaining $40,000, or $2,256.

SHOP AROUND FOR A 529

Nearly every state offers a 529, and you can use any one. If your state offers a tax deduction for contributions, however, you should probably choose that plan.

Choose the direct plan not the advisor-sold version, to save on fees. If you're not comfortable choosing investments, put all your money in the age-based option, which will get more conservative as your child approaches college age.

If in doubt, put your money in Utah's direct plan. It has rock-bottom fees and well-diversified age-based Vanguard mutual funds.

If you have a college tuition in your future, spend some quality time at **savingforcollege.com,** the most comprehensive source of information on 529 plans.

TERM LIFE INSURANCE vs PERMANENT LIFE

There are few financial topics as fraught with emotion—and profit motive—as life insurance. Strip away both, and the topic is fairly straightforward.

What is the purpose of life insurance? To provide for your dependents in the event of your death. Think about what would happen if your family no longer had your income. Odds are it would be financially devastating. If you have no dependents relying on your income, you do not need life insurance.

How much do you need? You need a policy big enough that your dependents can invest the payout and get enough income to cover those expenses you're no longer around to pay for. That's probably a big number. Assuming a 4 percent withdrawal rate, you'd need a $1 million policy to generate $40,000 in annual income.

How long should the policy last? Until your dependents will be independent. **Your youngest child's college graduation would be a sensible target date.**

So what kind of policy do you need? You need a **TERM POLICY**, which, as the name implies, will cover you for a set period. A smart strategy would be to buy a 20- or 25-year level-term policy upon the birth of your first child. "Level term" means the premiums won't change. I pay a little less than $1,000 a year for a million in term coverage that will last until I'm 61. What if I die at age 62? That would be unfortunate, but my kids will be out of college and my wife will inherit all my retirement savings, which I will no longer need. My family is covered.

Now, for most readers, the above sounds quite reasonable. But insurance salesmen will have steam coming out of their ears. A salesman will try to sell you **permanent life insurance,** which never expires and will pay out whenever you die. He will tell you that life insurance is an investment and tout its many benefits, including the fact that payout is tax free. Of course, unless your estate is north of $5 million, your heirs won't pay a federal estate tax, but never mind. And that $1 million of term coverage I have? If it were whole life, it would cost me $17,000 a year. Most people can't afford that, so they buy less. If they die young, they leave their dependents without enough coverage. Others buy the policy, then can't afford to keep up with the premiums.

The reason salesmen love these policies is that they pay enormous commissions. As much as 20 percent of the first year's premium could go to costs and commissions. Take, for instance, a product that salesmen love: single-premium whole life. Pay $100,000 and the salesman makes $20,000! And every year the salesman and his company get a little bit off the top. No wonder he loves this product.

This entire book is not long enough to rebut the multitude of arguments a practiced salesman will make. The bottom line is this: Permanent life insurance is a lousy investment for 99 percent of the population. (It's a great tax shelter for the wealthiest 1 percent, however.) If a salesman convinces you otherwise, take the policy he wants to sell you to a fee-only financial advisor who gets paid the same no matter what you invest in. Invite the salesman to the consultation. He'll probably decline.

DISABILITY INSURANCE vs LIFE INSURANCE

A wise friend once told me: *Dead men don't need incomes. Disabled ones do.*

Okay, this isn't really an either/or. Some people need both. But here's the key point: While you are more likely to *have* life insurance, you are more likely to *need* disability insurance. Estimates vary, but by one count, 20 percent of Americans will be disabled for a year or more during their working years.

And while you may think of disability as the construction worker collecting a check because of a bad back, that's actually the exception. Rather than workplace injuries, it's actually chronic diseases such as cancer, diabetes, or heart disease, or a musculoskeletal condition like arthritis that most often render people unable to earn a living.

You may have disability insurance through your employer, and you probably studied the policy about as carefully as you read the agreement the last time your iPod software updated. Worse, you might have declined the additional deduction because *you're a gather-ye-rosebuds-while-ye-may* type. Get that policy and check it out. If your employer doesn't offer a policy through work, you should purchase one. Here are three key things to look for in your work plan, or to

shop for if your employer either doesn't offer disability insurance or the one it does is inadequate.

- How much does the policy pay? The typical payout is 60 percent of your income; consider that the minimum necessary.

- Do you have short-term disability, long-term, or both? Short-term is designed to cover you if an illness keeps you out of work for a few weeks or a few months. That's helpful, but long-term care—which kicks in later and should cover you until retirement age—is crucial.

- How does the policy define disability? The best policies define disability as an injury that prevents you from doing your own job. Others, called "Any-Occ" policies, pay benefits only if you are incapable of doing *any* job.

If you do find yourself shopping for a long-term policy, you'll save on premiums by getting one with a longer waiting period before benefits kick in. Yes, that could mean you'd be without income for a while, but if you have a family support structure or enough savings to carry you over, that seems like a good tradeoff.

CASH-BACK CREDIT CARDS vs TRAVEL REWARDS CARDS

The credit card business is mind-bogglingly profitable. Even after paying for those ads you see everywhere, Visa earns close to $4 billion a year. It keeps more than 40 cents on every dollar of revenue that comes in — a profit margin that is the envy of many businesses.

Your goal as a consumer: to contribute as little as possible to those profits. I have nothing against Visa, MasterCard, or American Express. I am a customer of all three. But credit cards are different from almost any product you use. You cannot have a mortgage, a flat-screen TV, or a box of Cheerios without forking over cash. You can, however, have a credit card for free. Or you can pay interest, fees, and assorted charges and boost Visa's margins. Your call.

CASH-BACK

Rewards cards offer various perks that get bigger the more you spend. Cash-back cards generally pay you back about 1 percent of your purchases. Travel rewards cards give you points toward airline tickets or hotel stays, and sometimes let you cash in your points for merchandise. Cash back tends to be the better deal; you can always set aside that money and buy airline tickets if you want to.

Here's what you need to know:

1. If you do carry a balance, don't get a rewards card. They charge higher interest rates, and you'll pay far more in interest than you'll ever get in rewards. Your only goal is to get the card with the lowest possible rate. Once you've banished the balance, then consider a rewards card.

2. Don't get a card with an annual fee unless you are a really big spender who racks up so many rewards that they dwarf the fee.

3. If you go for airline miles, you're generally better off with cards that offer generic miles rather than signing up for an affinity card connected with a particular airline. Those miles are subject to blackout dates, and you are at the mercy of the airline to free up seats for miles redemption. Cash back tends to be the best deal. At the time of this writing, Capital One offered a 1.5 percent cash-back card. Though a Southwest Airlines Visa and a Starwood American Express card beat that deal by a hair, it's rare to find that kind of return on a card that gives you airline miles. (And if

you don't fly Southwest or stay in Sheratons, Westins, or Ws, you're out of luck.) Plus air miles have all sorts of potential disadvantages: They can expire, the rules constantly change, and, at least with affinity cards, it's easier to get Super Bowl tickets than to redeem your miles for seats on the flight you want. Cash, on the other hand, is cash.

There are more than 14 trillion airline miles in circulation. That sounds to me like a currency ripe for debasement.

Even though I know better, however, I collect miles rather than cash. My wife and I recently had an exquisite vacation at a resort called Parrot Cay in the Turks and Caicos islands. Using generic miles at the last minute, I got us direct flights on the precise days we wanted, and the sense of flying for "free" was fantastic.

ANNUAL VACATION

VS

NEW CAR

VACATION

Behavioral finance teaches us how emotion and other irrational forces play a huge, and largely unconscious, role in our decision-making process whenever money is at stake. It is fascinating stuff because it tells us a lot about what makes us happy, and it's counterintuitive. You'd think that buying a car, which you will have for years, would give you more pleasure than a week's vacation.

But some of the best authors on this topic, including Dan Ariely (*Predictably Irrational*) and Jason Zweig (*Your Money and Your Brain*), have explained that the thrill of a new possession wears off quickly. Just as our eyes adapt to bright sunlight when we go outside, or the smell of fresh air fades into the background, the car just becomes our ride. It's called hedonic adaptation, and it's why, no matter what we have, we always want more.

Spend a few days mountain biking up mesas in Moab, on the other hand, and you are mainlining new experiences that light up the pleasure centers of your brain. Whatever turns you on—lounging on a beach in the Virgin Islands, or exploring 2,000-year-old cobblestone streets in Naples—it won't last long enough to become mundane.

And even when it's over…it's really not. The memories of the trip will continue to give you pleasure long after you're back home, commuting to work in that old SUV. And here's the great thing about memories: They are uniquely yours. Nobody has a better one. Buy a new car, and, and, well, **whatever you drive home from the dealership will pale in comparison to Jay-Z's Bugatti.** But the way the sun floated above the horizon for that extra second just for the two of you, holding hands on a deserted beach? Nobody else has one of those.

BUY TRAVEL INSURANCE vs SAVE THE CASH

SAVE THE CASH

Travel insurance reimburses you if a trip is canceled or delayed, and covers damaged or lost property and emergency medical treatment.

In most cases, the smart financial move is to go without one of these policies. They are expensive—anywhere from 4 percent to 12 percent of the trip cost, depending on the policy—riddled with loopholes that may mean you aren't actually covered, and

may be redundant. For example, policies may have exclusions for epidemics or civil unrest—when riots broke out in Egypt, some travelers found they weren't covered. On the other hand, airlines will often change the rules to allow you to cancel a flight, as they did after the swine flu outbreak in Mexico. I was scheduled to fly to Boston shortly after 9/11, and my wife told me in no uncertain terms that I was not getting on a plane. Delta refunded the ticket with no questions asked. Some travel insurance policies will only allow you to cancel your flight if the terrorist attack occurs in your destination city.

YOUR HEALTH INSURANCE MAY STOP AT THE BORDER

Just because you take a pass on travel insurance, however, doesn't mean you shouldn't make sure you've got dengue fever coverage. Before heading overseas, check with your health insurance provider to make sure your policy covers you when you are overseas. Get a phone number for the company's call center, so you are prepared for an emergency. And if you happen to be taking Grannie along, keep this in mind: Medicare does not cover medical costs in other countries. You may want to take out a policy to cover her for the trip. Compare prices at SquareMouth.com.

BIG EXCEPTION #2
FLAKY FRIENDS & FAMILY

Travel plans are a rare case where you have knowledge that gives you an advantage over the insurance company. You've booked Disney for spring break, but you know that a sick relative could take a turn for the worse at any time. Or your little softball pitcher might make the travel team and have to stay home for a big game. Suddenly the risk/reward proposition of a "cancel for any reason" policy looks a lot more favorable.

BIG EXCEPTION #1
WEATHER

The beachfront bungalow you've picked out for your honeymoon is paradise on Earth. But it's right in the middle of hurricane alley. Forget the economics, this is a case where it's worth overpaying to protect yourself. As the waves wash away your dreams, your new bride really doesn't want to hear that you read in some financial book that travel insurance was overpriced. Step up and buy a "cancel for any reason" policy—it's more expensive, but, as the name suggests, you're covered. Compare policies at SquareMouth.com or InsureMyTrip.com.

EXTENDED WARRANTY vs SELF INSURE

Whether you are buying a mutual fund or a flat-screen TV, there are two components to the price you pay. The cost of the item, and the fees and commission to the people selling it to you. Much of this book is devoted to minimizing that second number.

So it's useful to know that **retailers often make more money by selling you an extended warranty than they make on the product itself.** That should tell you a lot about who's getting the better deal on the warranty. Hint: It's not you.

Here's the bottom line: The odds are that whatever you purchase will not break down during the period covered by the warranty. The best financial move is to **self insure.** When the salesman offers you the warranty, ask what it will cost. Then politely, but firmly, decline.

As soon as you get home, transfer the cost of the warranty into a savings account. You might even set up a separate online account for this purpose. If you do this for every gadget and appliance you purchase, you'll find the account fills up pretty fast. If something breaks, use that account to repair or replace it—without worrying about a warranty's fine print. If nothing breaks, hey, you keep the money instead of Best Buy.

To improve your odds, check your credit card agreements to see which one has the most generous warranty extension policy. Some cards will double a one-year manufacturer's warranty. In fact Costco does that automatically on TVs.

And once you're covered for two years, the warranty window starts to get pretty narrow. Unless the product breaks *after* 24 months but *before* 36 months, you wasted your money on a three-year warranty.

With cars, the same rules apply. A *Consumer Reports* survey found that, on average, buyers spent $1,000 for coverage and received $700 in benefits. More than 40 percent never used the coverage at all.

If you put a high value on the peace of mind that comes with a warranty, then consider using it only when the price of the item is so high that replacing it would cause a lot of pain. Pass when you buy a cell phone or microwave, pay up for the warranty when you invest in a plasma TV.

MARY ANN vs GINGER

Don't even think about it, pal. You want to really bring your personal economy crashing down? Your own mini Lehman Brothers collapse? Then stray from your marriage.

STAY FAITHFUL

I'm not going to cover the non-financial aspects of divorce here, and I'm not suggesting that you should ride out a failed marriage for economic reasons. But few events can torpedo your financial plan like a divorce. Think about your monthly mortgage payment—it's probably a significant number, right? If your household becomes two households, add a rent payment on top of that. New couch, new bed, a second utility bill. With only one person in the house, childcare just got more expensive. Oh, and you'll each be writing a check to an attorney.

Since I'm sporting both an X and a Y chromosome, I can't help but come at the subject of divorce from a male perspective. So, dads, be warned: Whether it's a one-night stand or you take up with a really nice lady who is destined to be your second soul mate, the legal system does not look kindly on you. Your child support obligations will not stop just because your wife meets a nice millionaire. And you may go to jail if you fail to meet those obligations. Even the tax code smiles on your ex-wife. Unlike alimony, those support payments are not tax deductible for you, but if your wife has custody, she gets the "head of household" benefits on her tax return. Plus she can take a $1,000-per-child tax credit in 2012, even if you're supporting the kids. And, while state laws vary, you can assume that if you've got $500,000 in a retirement account and your wife didn't work, you can say good-bye to $250,000.

Yes, it requires work to keep a marriage running smoothly. But here's some man-to-man advice. To all the other reasons that you stay faithful to your wife, add one more: a single night's slipup could easily cost you a million bucks over your lifetime. Now, go tell your wife to sit down. You'll clean up the dishes.

LONG-TERM CARE INSURANCE vs FLY SOLO

Long-term care may be the most difficult insurance decision you face. As with all insurance, the variables are unknowable—the problem is that in this case you pay a stiff penalty for guessing wrong.

Long-term care insurance is designed to pay for day-to-day help you may need as you age. It's a wide range—could be 24/7 care, or perhaps nothing more than some help cooking and getting out of the bathtub. It can be expensive compared with, say, term life insurance. (A 55-year-old might pay $2,000 a year for a decent LTC policy.) But the odds that you'll need it are higher. Unlike life insurance, which is quite straightforward—you die, your beneficiary gets paid—long-term care is squishier. Definitions of care vary, so some policies may not cover your desired provider. Insurance companies have been known to resist making payouts, forcing their elderly policyholders into a battle they are ill prepared to fight. And if you do need care, how long will you need it? The longer the period guaranteed by the policy, the higher the premiums.

A few statistics illustrate the problem:

A landmark study found that more than half of people turning 65 would face little or no costs for long-term care. But more than 15 percent would face costs ranging from $100,000 to more than $250,000—and that's not accounting for inflation. A year of service from a home health aide will run you more than $188,000 in Missouri by 2040, according to a calculator from insurance provider Genworth. An assisted living facility would cost almost as much.

Another uncomfortable unknown: Unlike level-term life insurance, long-term care premiums can go up. So it's tough to budget for them.

Here's how to make the best of a bad hand: If you have significant assets—I mean a minimum of $1 million in retirement savings plus home equity north of $500,000, you may be able to self insure. Should you need care, you may be able to pay for it out of pocket, plus you'll have real estate flexibility—a loan against your house, or a reverse mortgage, or an outright sale. That said, some wealthy couples buy insurance anyway to protect their portfolio. In the worst case, one spouse needs, say, five years of expensive care, and the other spouse lives another 25 years, but has no money left.

If you're not wealthy, buy a policy that will pay for three years of care, which will be less expensive than a policy that guarantees coverage for as long as you need it. A long-term care association study found that only 8 percent of 106,000 customers making claims exhausted the benefits of three-year policies.

When shopping for a plan, check the insurance company's rating at thestreet.com, moodys.com, and standardandpoors.com. For added protection, **only consider companies with decades of history selling LTC—Genworth, Prudential, and Northwestern Mutual are the big players.** You'll want a plan with flexibility, so that home health care, adult day care, assisted living facilities, residential care, and nursing homes are all covered.

Buy a policy in your 50s, which is early enough that you should be healthy and get a decent rate. And let your kids know that you're spending big bucks to ensure that their guest room never becomes Paw-Paw's Pee-Pee Palace.

ALLOWANCE VS PAY FOR CHORES

There's a bit of a debate—at least among people who worry about this stuff—over whether to give kids an allowance just for being your children, or whether to make them work for the money.

ALLOWANCE PLUS

For me the answer is simple: One of the most important financial lessons to pass on to your children is how to make choices and set priorities. It's easy for them to hector you into buying them plastic princess figurines and other kiddie crap that will end up as nighttime land mines in your living room. But if they have to part with their own limited funds, they are forced to weigh the relative merits of firefly stickers compared with Sour Patch Kids. That's a crucial skill.

So for starters, give your children a small allowance. **Experts recommend a range between half and twice a child's age in dollars.** You decide whether your six-year-old should have $3 or $12 or something in between, **but don't tie it to chores.** Instead, teach your children that certain tasks are simply part of being a household; after all they won't get paid for making their bed as adults.

One popular approach is to divide the allowance into thirds: one dollar for spending, one for saving, and one for charity. You can even find piggy banks with three compartments.

My seven-year-old daughter thought long and hard about whether a little stuffed penguin at the Central Park Zoo was worth $8 in birthday money. After a consultation with Dad (she called me at the office), she decided to go for it, and she clearly values Penny the Penguin more highly because she paid for it herself.

Now, the pay-for-chores crowd says the "free" allowance doesn't teach kids the value of hard work. True. So offer your children the chance to make more money for taking on tougher tasks—weeding the garden, say, or painting the garage. If they do a job that you might have otherwise hired someone to do, well, I see a win-win in the making.

As children get older, it's particularly important to set up ground rules for what expenditures are their responsibility, so they learn to budget for them. By the time they are college sophomores, they should have a debit card that gives them access to a whole semester's spending money. They will see the balance shrink every time they pull out the plastic, and you must make it clear to them that when it's gone, it's gone. *There are no bailouts in this family.*

If they can learn that lesson, they'll be one step ahead of Congress.

ORGANIC FRUITS & VEGETABLES vs CONVENTIONAL

I was staring at the strawberries for a long time.

One pack was $3.99, the other was $4.99.

I could not see any difference in the fruit. The more expensive package, of course, was organic.

Am I a bad dad if I bring home the cheaper box?

Am I a sucker if I spring for the pesticide-free?

KNOW THE DIRTY DOZEN

Whole Foods got the nickname "whole paycheck," for a reason, and the high-cost of organic foods is partly to blame.

Your best strategy is to pay up for organic when it comes to the "Dirty Dozen," the fruits and vegetables that had the most pesticide residue according to an analysis of Department of Agriculture tests by the Environmental Working Group. The group found that eating the 12 most contaminated fruits and vegetables will expose a person to about 15 pesticides a day, on average. Eating the 12 least contaminated will expose a person to fewer than two pesticides a day.

There are also advantages to choosing organic milk, eggs, and meat, largely because they have more omega-3 fatty acids. And while the whole organic thing may sound like a yuppie fad, remember that it's actually the food your grandparents ate, before factory farms and pesticides. Cows that live outside in the sun and eat grass, for example, produce steak with vastly more nutrients—it's that simple.

ORGANIC

peaches

apples

bell peppers

celery

nectarines

strawberries

cherries

pears

imported grapes

spinach

lettuce

potatoes

DON'T PAY UP

corn

peas

onions

avocados

mangoes

asparagus

kiwis

bananas

broccoli

cabbage

eggplants

papayas

HIRE A TRAINER vs GO IT ALONE

Splurge on the trainer.

If you belong to a gym, an excellent financial exercise is to divide your annual membership fee by the number of times you go. It may shock you how much you are paying per visit.

WHO NEEDS A BRICK-AND-MORTAR GYM?

Who needs a brick-and-mortar gym? To get in shape, you need motivation and expertise. Fire the gym and use that money to hire a trainer who will run you through the paces in a local park. Beware: Anyone, including your cat, can get "certified" as a trainer with an online course. Coopersmith says to look for at least one of these sets of letters, which are reputable outfits: NSCA, ACSM, ACE, NASM, or NCSF.

The median annual cost of a new gym membership is $775, so if you go only twice a month, that's $32 a workout. The standard financial advice would be to drop that membership. But a gym is different from an underutilized Netflix account. Even infrequent bouts on the Stairmaster have some health benefits. My advice: Pay more, but get a lot more value in return, by hiring a trainer.

For years I went to the gym only when the weather was too awful for running. I didn't know what I was doing, so just used the same machines and free weights that I had used in high school. Over 10 years I'd spent more than $10,000 on gym dues, and didn't have a whole lot to show for it.

So I hired a trainer at an Equinox health club, and, at nearly 40 years old, I lowered my body fat, put on 10 pounds of muscle, and repaired a back injury. When you hire a trainer, suddenly the gym goes from the bottom of your priority list to a rectangle on your Outlook calendar. You show up, and you work hard for an hour.

One of a trainer's jobs is to get you out of your comfort zone, explains Geralyn Coopersmith, who's in charge of training the trainers at Equinox. **"People tend to gravitate toward the thing that they are best at,** so skinny people run and flexible people do yoga, and big strong guys lift," she says. **"But usually they need the thing that they find least appealing, because that fixes their weak link."** And by focusing on what you really need, you get the results you were looking for in the first place.

For me, the benefits didn't stop when the training sessions were done. Now I go to the gym more frequently, and make much better use of my time there. I have an arsenal of exercises that I learned from the trainers, so instead of doing the same routine each visit, I mix it up, which is more interesting and, many studies have shown, produces better results. In other words, I'm getting a lot more brawn for my buck.

If you don't think you can afford training sessions plus a gym membership, create your own layaway plan. Quit your gym now, but keep making payments—to yourself. Deposit the monthly dues in a savings account until you have enough to pay for the sessions. Meanwhile, share your plan with the manager of your gym. Once he knows what you are doing, he may cut you a deal on the membership if you are willing to pay for the sessions up front.

VI. RETIREMENT

"JUST PUT ME ON AN ICE FLOE" IS NOT A STRATEGY

Many of the financial challenges addressed in this book—paying for college, buying a house—have been around for generations. And while they haven't gotten any easier to master, you do have a few tools your parents didn't have, such as 529 college savings plans and extremely low mortgage rates.

In the case of supporting yourself through retirement, however, it's the other way around. You face retirement challenges that no other generation has ever seen, and some of the tools your parents had are going away. If your father worked for a big, or even medium-size, company, odds are he retired with a pension—a guaranteed income stream for life. Today, corporate pensions are melting away faster than the polar ice cap.

Social Security, despite some scary headlines and political grandstanding, is unlikely to go away. But it may shrink. To understand where the program is headed, it helps to clear up one common misunderstanding—there is no trust fund. It's a pay-as-you-go system. Our Social Security taxes pay for our parents' benefits, and we hope our kids' taxes will support us. The problem is demographics—as the population ages, there are fewer young workers to support each retiree. To survive in the long term, the system needs more income (read: higher taxes) and lower benefits, and we'll probably see both in the coming decades.

On top of your nonexistent pension and your potentially lower Social Security benefits, consider this: Your genera-tion is going to need more money in retirement than your parents did because life spans are increasing. If you are in good health, it's quite possible you'll live well into your 90s. That means you'll need to save enough money to support yourself for 30 years or more.

It's hard to overstate how awesome a responsibility you have been saddled with, and how unprepared most people are to tackle it. First, you have to accumulate a serious sum. And then you need to manage that money with great skill, so you don't outlive your cash.

Step number one: Save till it hurts. Use an online calcula-tor to size up your needs—T. Rowe Price and Fidelity both have good ones. And while you're crunching numbers, think about how you want to spend your days after you give up the nine-to-five. If you've got something to look forward to, you might find it's a little easier to dump all that money into your 401(k) every two weeks.

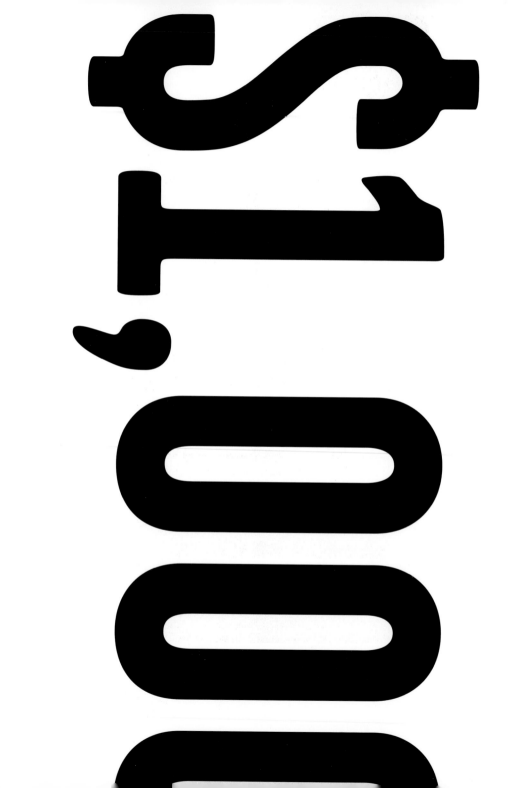

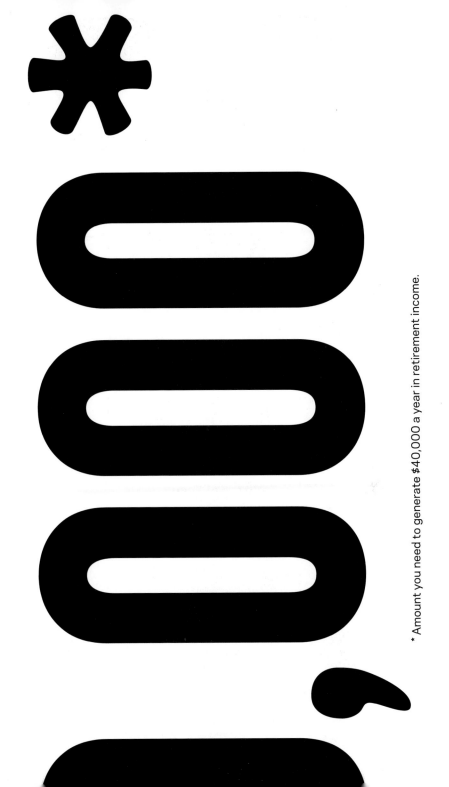

*Amount you need to generate $40,000 a year in retirement income.

SAVE FOR YOUR KIDS' COLLEGE
vs SAVE FOR YOUR RETIREMENT

PAY YOURSELF FIRST

Pay yourself first. That's a good rule for just about any financial decision, but it's tough to follow when it means denying your kids. Here's a good way to think about it: Would you rather spend your 20s and 30s paying off student loans, or your 40s and 50s with your destitute parents living in your guest room? That's an easy call for you, and it'll be just as easy for your kids.

It's not that paying for college is easy, it's that paying for retirement is so damn hard. With college, you have options: You can send your children to less expensive state universities; they can win scholarships, apply for financial aid, or secure low-interest loans. None of that help exists for retirement—it's all up to you.

Your parents' retirement is probably supported by a three-legged stool: pension, Social Security, and personal savings. That stool has been kicked out from under you. Pensions are something your dad got but you don't. The Social Security Trust Fund reserves are expected to be exhausted in 2037. (Although there will still be enough to guarantee some payouts, and taxes will probably be hiked to pay for continued benefits.) And savings rates have plummeted since 1980—by some estimates they hovered near zero for years before ticking higher during the Great Recession.

Oh, and you need a lot more money than your parents did, because you'll live longer. In 1960, life expectancy was 69.8, today it's 78.4. And if you're healthy and your genes are cooperative, you could easily live into your 90s.

Follow the advice of the flight attendant: Put on your oxygen mask before putting on your child's. You're no use to the kids if you can't breathe.

529 RULES OF THUMB

- Always use the "direct plan," not the "broker-sold" plan; you'll pay much less in expenses. If you're not comfortable making investing decisions on your own, switch on autopilot by choosing the "target date" or "age-based" fund, which automatically moves your money into more conservative investments as your child gets closer to freshman year.

- You are not required to use the plan from your home state, but if your state offers a tax deduction for 529 deposits, you're probably better off using it.

- If your state does not offer a tax deduction, shop around for the plan with the lowest expenses and the best investment options. If in doubt, go with Utah. The plan uses low-cost Vanguard index funds and charges rock-bottom fees.

While saving for retirement needs to be your first priority, you should still save for your kids' college education if you can possibly afford it. So after you max out your 401(k), learn three more numbers: 529.

529 plans are an incredible gift from the IRS. You put money in the plan and all the growth is tax-free as long as you use it for college expenses. Some states even give you a state tax deduction for the money you save. That's an even sweeter deal than a Roth IRA, and, unlike the Roth, there is no income limit on a 529.

ROTH IRA vs TRADITIONAL IRA

GO ROTH

There are many confusing rules surrounding individual retirement accounts (IRAs), but here's the basic choice you face: **With a Roth IRA, you pay taxes on the money now, and then pay no taxes when you withdraw your cash and the gains during retirement.** With a traditional IRA, you can deduct your contributions now, but when you retire you pay tax on the money.

So the standard financial advice is that if you expect higher taxes when you retire, go for the Roth, while if you expect your tax rate will go down, go the traditional route. I don't like that advice, for two reasons. First, it requires a lot of guesswork. In addition to correctly estimating what your retirement income will be, you have to know what tax rates will be in 20 or 30 or 40 years.

Here's my take: By making the maximum contribution to a Roth (**which is named for the late Delaware Senator William V. Roth, Jr.**) you are saving more money for retirement than if you max out a traditional IRA. Why? Because you are paying the tax now, and you'll get to keep 100 cents of every dollar in that account. With a traditional IRA, you'll have to give 10 or 20 or 25 cents of every dollar to Uncle Sam as you make withdrawals.

Make no mistake: Since you're putting *after-tax* dollars into the Roth, you have to earn roughly $1.25 (depending on your tax bracket) for every buck you invest. But consider the human element; what some economists call behavioral finance. When we have money, we tend to spend it. As our cash flow increases, lo and behold, our expenses always seem to grow right along with it. So if you divert that money straight into a Roth, you may not miss it. But once you're retired and on a fixed income, you'll thank the younger you for prepaying those taxes.

ROTH LIMITS & OPTIONS

There are income limits above which you cannot contribute directly to a Roth IRA or deduct IRA contributions. For the 2011 tax year (the return you file in April 2012) the limits were $179,000 (married filing jointly) and $122,000 (single). There is an option for big earners however: Anyone can convert a traditional IRA to a Roth. You just have to pay taxes on any untaxed money within the traditional IRA (such as earnings and any deductible contributions).

FIXED ANNUITY vs VARIABLE ANNUITY

FIXED

You don't have to spend very long as a business journalist before you realize that the worse a financial product, the fiercer its defenders. The phenomenon is easy to explain: What makes the product bad is that it transfers your wealth to the salesman. That's why he loves it!

Few products better illustrate this reality than variable annuities. For most people, in most situations, they are lousy financial products. I'll explain why below, but maybe all you need to know is this: Insurance brokers push these things harder than a car salesman trying to get last year's model off the lot. Fee-only advisors, on the other hand, who get paid the same regardless of what they recommend, rarely suggest them to clients.

In short, **variable annuities** are insurance products that come with an investment component. They often guarantee that your original investment will be returned in full. The return is based on some underlying investment, such as a stock mutual fund. The returns are tax deferred until you withdraw them. You can often choose to "annuitize" them, which means you withdraw regular payments over a specified amount of time.

A **fixed immediate annuity** is a much duller, simpler, and better product. **You give the insurance company a lump sum, and it makes fixed payments back to you for a specified time, usually the rest of your life.** Fixed annuities solve a real problem: By guaranteeing an income stream for as long as you live, they ensure you don't run out of money before you die.

So, for instance, if you retire at 67 with $900,000 in your 401(k), you might take half that money and purchase fixed immediate annuities from low-cost providers. You'd get a total payout of around $28,000 a year for the rest of your life.

Notice I used the plural for "annuities." That's because state insurance regulators generally insure annuity investments of up to $100,000 to protect you in case the issuer defaults, so you shouldn't invest more than $100,000 with any single company. Also, today's extremely low interest rates mean that annuity payouts are lower, so I'd recommend waiting to annuitize if possible, and consider opting for an annuity that increases payouts according to inflation.

Variable annuities, on the other hand, address problems that can usually be solved less expensively with other products, and sometimes they solve problems you don't have. For instance if someone tries to sell you a variable annuity within an IRA, they are trying to charge you for a tax benefit the IRA already provides.

So why are variable annuities bad?

First, the fees range from large to enormous. In most cases you'll pay a commission of 5 percent or more when you invest. That's $500 on a $10,000 investment. There are also annual fees charged by the insurance company, plus the mutual funds in variable annuities usually charge higher fees than the low-cost funds you could buy outside of annuities.

Second, your money is locked up for years: Most companies charge a surrender fee if you take the money out or change investments within the first 5 to 10 years of the contract.

Finally, the benefit of the tax deferral is diluted because you pay income tax on earnings, rather than the lower capital gains tax rate you would pay if you simply owned the mutual fund in a taxable account.

FIXED ANNUITY vs MANAGED PAYOUT FUND

FIXED ANNUITY

I've written about a couple of risks you need to address to ensure a comfortable retirement: market risk (stocks plummet) and inflation risk (your dollar buys less). But even if you lick those two, there's another you've got to protect against. Planners call it longevity risk. I call it "running out of money before you die."

Your dad may have had a pension—in 1975, 70 percent of employees did. Today, 21 percent of nonunion employees have one and the number is falling, which means you are more likely to get a customer service representative who speaks English than have a guaranteed income stream in retirement.

To address this problem, the financial industry has rolled out a number of new products in recent years. One of the more interesting is the managed payout fund, also known as a retirement income fund. Essentially they are mutual funds that send you regular checks. Generally they are "funds of funds," which means they are actually comprised of a bunch of underlying mutual funds that each focus on different assets, such as stocks, bonds, or commodities. Most aim to preserve your principal, though Fidelity's are designed to liquidate by a certain date; say 20 years from the time you invest. They are sometimes referred to as "target-death funds" (well, not by Fidelity).

These funds are similar to a fixed annuity in that they provide you with income, but the big difference is that they don't come with a guarantee. An **annuity**, remember, is a contract with an insurance company: You give the company a big lump sum and it guarantees you a certain payout for the rest of your life. (Most states insure you against default up to $100,000 per account.)

A managed payout fund has some advantages over a fixed annuity—your investment can grow, and you can sell and withdraw your money at any time. And you could do a lot worse than having the pros at Vanguard or Fidelity manage your retirement income. But what's dangerous is the *implied* guarantee that these things will send you a check forever. There is no guarantee, and one of Vanguard's funds lost 30 percent in 2008, when the market crashed.

Bottom line: Don't substitute a managed payout fund for an annuity; they serve different purposes. Strongly consider an annuity to ensure you don't run out of money. Then, if you have a solid financial plan for retirement, you're probably better off skipping the managed payout fund and building a diversified portfolio of low-cost index funds that serves the same role, but at zero cost.

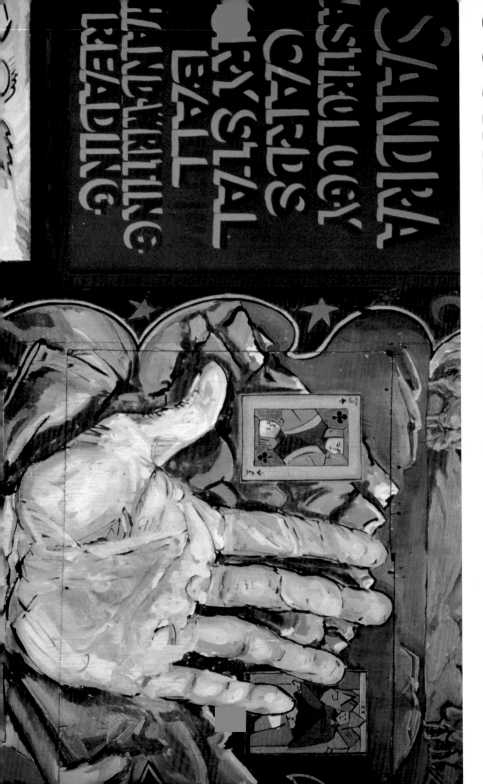

SOCIAL SECURITY AT 62 vs 70

WAIT UNTIL 70

Maximizing your Social Security benefits can have a huge impact on your quality of life as a retiree, and the strategies for doing so can get very complicated. But there is one golden rule that everyone should understand: The longer you wait to file for Social Security the bigger your monthly check. And the difference between taking it at 62 versus taking it at 70 is huge. Huge as in, nearly double.

Consider the numbers: Say you are making $75,000 and retire in 2012 at age 62. Your estimated annual payout would be $16,300 (it varies depending on lifetime earnings). If you wait until your "full retirement age" of 66, your yearly Social Security income would be roughly $22,600. And if you hold off until age 70? $30,250.

You'll hear people say you should take your checks early and invest them. Assuming you have the discipline to follow that plan, the odds are still against you. Every year you wait, your Social Security payout increases by 8 percent. To match that return in the market would require luck, skill, and, this is very important, a lot of risk. There's no such thing as a guaranteed 8 percent annual return. Why take the risk to get something the government will hand you? Of course some people cannot afford to wait. But if you can, think carefully about the decision.

Holding out for the bigger paycheck gets more valuable the longer you live. Using the numbers in the example above, if you live to age 90, you will have received $170,000 more in Social Security by waiting until age 70 to take benefits. (There's no benefit to waiting past age 70.)

Clearly, life expectancy plays a role in your decision. If you are in poor health, you may weigh these numbers differently. You can get an estimate of your life expectancy at the website livingto100.com. Once you have a number, play around with the calculators at Social Security.gov.

Making this decision requires you to estimate when you're going to die, which is depressing, and also unknowable. But consider the two risks. The first is that you die young and collect less in benefits. The other is that you live to a ripe old age, but your Social Security checks are inadequate. I'd rather protect against the second one. If it turns out I made the wrong decision, I won't be around to feel bad about it.

YOUR OWN SOCIAL SECURITY
BENEFITS vs YOUR SPOUSE'S

BOTH

Just when you and your soon to be sunset-years-entering spouse have exhausted the usual subjects of conversation (Why do the kids always kick the Tanqueray without replacing it? The neighbors—where do they get all that money?), here comes the hot topic of Social Security benefits. Okay, so it's not a little blue pill or Jell-O-covered Twister, but it does have a certain appeal. It gives you the chance to think of your relationship as spouses with benefits.

Under the rules of Social Security, the lower-earning spouse can take either her* own benefits or half of her husband's, whichever is greater. So that's a fairly easy choice.

Here's where it gets tricky: While there is a huge advantage to delaying Social Security benefits until age 70, there is no advantage to delaying spousal benefits past age 66. And you can't tap your spousal benefit until your spouse files for Social Security. So should a couple file spouse files for Social Security, or wait until age 70?

They can do both. The solution is called "file and suspend." The higher-earning spouse files for benefits but immediately suspends them. His wife is then qualified to start

receiving spousal benefits, and at age 70 he can then start pocketing the maximum benefit. If he dies, his wife will receive his full benefit.

It gets better: If both spouses worked full careers, their personal benefits are probably larger than half their spouse's benefit. But if the higher-earning spouse pulls the "file and suspend" maneuver, his spouse can start receiving spousal benefits. This means the couple has some income coming in, but it enables her to delay her own filing until age 70, when she can receive her maximum payout.

You can receive the spousal Social Security benefit even if you are divorced, as long as your marriage lasted at least 10 years.

To figure out the best strategy for maximizing benefits, check out the calculators at SocialSecurity.gov. It may even be worth hiring a financial planner with expertise in the topic. The right strategy could net you more than $100,000 over your retirement years, making the planner's fee an excellent investment.

---

* I apologize if the female pronoun offends; "his or her" gets tiresome, and, while it's not fair, the husband's income is usually the larger one in the generation that is on the cusp of retirement today.

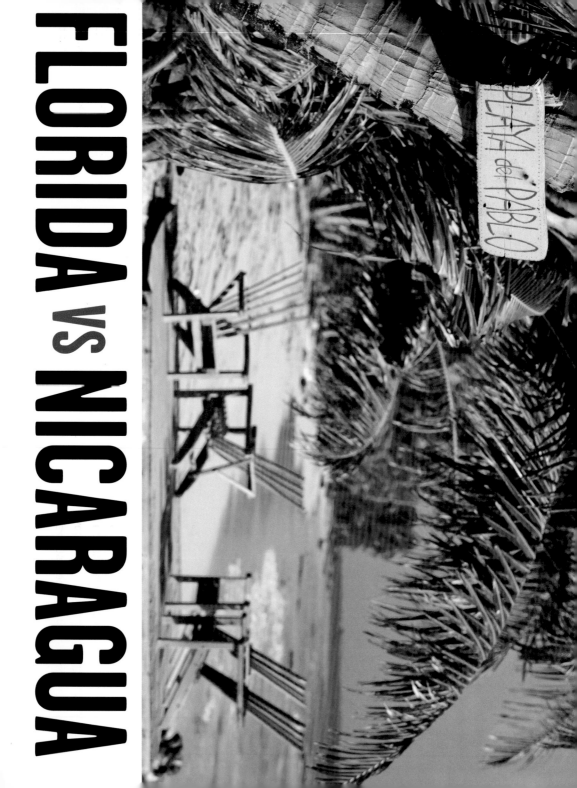

FLORIDA vs NICARAGUA

A 50-something woman in New York hired a financial advisor to help her answer a common question—she wanted to know when she would be able to retire. He carefully analyzed her income and expenses, and came up with a precise answer: Never.

At least not in New York, where she had a mortgage and sky-high living costs. Luckily, she had a plan B. Since she had family in Mexico, she asked when she could retire south of the border. This time his answer was quicker: Tomorrow. She started packing.

It's impossible to generalize about the prices, but for anywhere from $10,000 (for 10 acres in Argentina) to $500,000 (water-front home in Panama) you can find property that most people would never be able to afford in the lower 48. Prices are already climbing—Costa Rica is getting expensive.

A couple of rules before you the make leap:

- Get a calendar and write an imaginary schedule for every day for an entire month of retirement. You can't spend *all* your time golfing and reading books. (This is an excellent exercise for anyone planning retirement.)

- Spend a lot of time at your potential destination. Rent an apartment for a two-week vacation. Talk to expats and ask about the downsides.

- If you get serious and start a property hunt, try to use a big global agency that has a local franchise, such as Sotheby's or Coldwell Banker. They have a reputation to uphold, they are used to dealing with Americans, and they can hook you up with other professionals you will need, such as lawyers, to help cut through any red tape

OPTIONS

A small but growing number of retirees—estimated at more than 500,000—are tapping their inner F. Scott Fitzgerald and heading overseas. The greenback goes a lot farther in Central and South America and in Eastern Europe, especially when it comes to real estate. Consider some alternatives:

ACTIVITY	WISHFUL THINKING	BRILLIANT ALTERNATIVE
Skiing the Alps	Switzerland	Romania
Visiting Wineries	Loire Valley	Mendoza, Argentina
Gazing at the Sea	Santa Barbara, California	Nicaragua or Panama

- If you buy property and plan to simply hold on to it for years or decades until retirement, hire a caretaker. Even if it's just vacant land, a squatter could settle down there and you might lose your rights to the property. Safer yet: Buy into a development that caters to expats.

ACKNOWLEDGMENTS

Joan Didion says that everyone lives "by the imposition of a narrative line upon disparate images." *Worth It . . . Not Worth It?* is the sum of my disparate images and would not have been possible without the help, guidance, and friendships of many.

The narrative begins in a household run by parents born in the 1930s. They learned lessons in the Great Depression, passed them on to me, and I have, in a well-meaning but imperfect way, tried to live by them. My father, also Jack Otter, still tells the story of how, at all of eight years old, I berated him for trying to buy cereal at one of our neighborhood grocery stores. My mother, Susan, had schooled me in comparison shopping, and so I explained to him that the market we were in had good prices on bread and milk, but that A&P was the place for buying packaged goods such as cereal.

The narrative line requires three more elements: writing, financial expertise, and the time to put a book together.

First, the ability to write. No one encouraged that more than my ninth-grade teacher, the late David King-Wood—an Oxford-educated British actor who spent the back half of his 89 years teaching English and French at New York's St. Bernard's School. I suspect DKW was more focused on potential than actual ability, God bless him, and the encouragement was enough to launch a career centered on words.

Helen Rattray, now publisher of *The East Hampton Star*, gave me a shot at covering just about every small-town beat there is, from

cops to schools to local government, and showed a unwavering commitment to journalistic ethics that impresses me even more now than it did back then. Somehow I caught the eye of Lenny Ackerman, an attorney whose radio station, WRMC, didn't quite work out as planned, but whose kindness to me allowed the painful, but necessary departure from small-town reporting. I was lucky enough to spend some time at the radio station with Peter Schellbach—who wisely got out of journalism before it was too late. Schellbach, now a bond-trader extraordinaire, tells me how things really work on Wall Street. If he and my mom were running things, the crash of '08 never would have happened.

At *Newsday*, Steve Sink and Rich Galant saw fit to rescue me from the copy desk and give me a gig on the business desk. I will be forever in their debt. Then came the wonderful headhunter Karen Danziger, who convinced Pete Finch to take a chance on me at *SmartMoney* magazine, right before the tech bubble burst. At *SmartMoney* my economics education got a boost from the late Jersey Gilbert, who peered at me from behind his desk, piled high with research, and delivered late-night lectures on everything from Keynesian theory to the business cycle to the best roads to take when driving through West Virginia. The first two were invaluable. While there, I was also lucky enough to "edit" Paul Sturm, which I imagine is like "editing" Joan Didion or "training" Usain Bolt. I am grateful for having had the opportunity to be his student, and plan to continue trying to coax him into writing for me again. The wisdom passed on by Fleming Meeks, now executive editor of *Barron's*, peppers this book. One of my best sources at *SmartMoney*—and ever since—was fee-only financial advisor Gary Schatsky, whose mission in life is to make sure you keep more of your money.

Next stop: Rodale, where Stephen Perrine taught me to hone service journalism until the advice was sharp enough to cut your thumb. I think this book is worth many times its cover price, and Steve deserves some credit for that. He also was kind enough to brainstorm titles, and I was inconsiderate enough to completely ignore his advice. On assignment from Steve, I interviewed my old friend Jerry Della Femina, who shared one of the most inspirational stories I've ever heard. I'll save the details for my next book, but when the task of writing this one seemed overwhelming, I reminded myself of the day Jerry walked miles through freezing weather for an interview that never happened.

Some of the most important insights you will gain from these pages I learned at the feet of Eric Schurenberg, now editor of Inc.com, and Allan Roth, a blogger and financial advisor. They, in turn, introduced me to a mutual fund executive who must remain anonymous because he has leaked secrets of his industry that you're not supposed to know. By sharing them here, I'm giving you the chance to keep money in your pocket instead of handing it over to his already over-compensated colleagues.

Before I wrap this up, I have to thank Dan Farber, editor of CBSNews.com, who had been my boss for about 10 seconds before I told him I needed to take a week off to work on *Worth It . . . Not Worth It?* Thanks for the vacation time, Dan.

Then there's Jon Stewart, who has absolutely nothing to do with this project, but whose show I would really like to go on to talk about it.

Now for the people who actually have sweat equity in the book you're holding. Television star, radio host, and financial expert Jill Schlesinger, along with Allan Roth, pored over the manuscript to catch errors and sharpen the advice. Thanks, guys. If a picture is worth a thousand words, designer Kevin Smith gets way more credit than I do for this book. My editor, John Brodie, didn't merely help shape the ideas, sharpen the language, and inspire those clever illustrations. He made it happen. The person for whom words are least adequate to fully explain her contribution is my wife, Diane. For every weekend I ran off to an empty house in the country to work, for every late night I stayed at the office to bang on the keyboard— indeed at the very moment I type these words, she is taking care of the family so I can write. A project like this is a zero-sum game; for every hour I spend on the laptop, my wife spends an hour doing a job I might otherwise be helping with. She encouraged me and repeatedly gave the all-important green light to keep it going. I really hope she likes it because I love her.

PHOTO CREDITS

ABOUT THE AUTHOR

Jack Otter is currently the executive editor of CBS Money Watch.com, and he has more than a decade of experience as a business journalist, having been on staff at *Newsday* and *SmartMoney*. He lives in Brooklyn, New York, with his wife and two children.

Follow him on Twitter @JackOtter.